A GUIDE TO PAINTING IN OILS

Barbara Dorf

This original and helpful book is designed to help anyone starting oil painting to create pictures that are entirely theirs. The general idea is to encourage everyone who reads it to express themselves in their own way. Rules that are given are only guides, and can be broken if the result is a good, individual painting.

Extensive information is given on the many aspects of oil painting materials and techniques. Brushes, varnishes, primings and supports are dealt with accurately but simply and advice is given on care and maintenance of equipment. The many line illustrations and diagrams in the text make points clearer and easier to follow.

The book is based on the author's considerable experience of teaching beginners at all levels in schools, colleges and art clubs. There is something for everyone who wishes to paint—abstract, landscape, portraits, etc. Oil painting is approached as something to give satisfaction and pleasure to both the painter and the onlooker.

It is with gratitude and pleasure that I acknowledge the unfailing kindness, encouragement and help from the following; Tom Rowney, G. Addison, at Rowney's, Artists' Colourmen; Dr. R. D. Harley, at Winsor & Newton, Artists' Colourmen; Michael Holmes, Chief Technician, The Slade Schools U.C.L.; L. S. Michael, Esq., O.B.E.; Bernard Dunstan, R.A.; Patricia A. Edmonds.

A Guide to Painting in Oils

BARBARA DORF

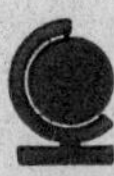

SPHERE BOOKS LIMITED
30/32 Gray's Inn Road, London WC1X 8JL

First published in Great Britain by Pelham Books Ltd 1971

First Sphere Books edition 1973
Reprinted 1977

TRADE
MARK

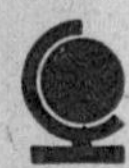

Set in Monotype Baskerville

Printed in Great Britain by
Hazell Watson & Viney Ltd
Aylesbury, Bucks

CONTENTS

CHAPTER ONE

A FEW WORDS TO START YOU OFF

Painting can be learned. Once you have the will to paint you can forget about whether you think you have the talent or not. At this stage, there is only one rule, that is having the courage to begin. It would be good if this book made it possible for the reader to make painting a spontaneous means of expression. Most of us, at some time, have responded to things in the external world, that have made us wish we could paint. This is as it should be, for it is natural for everyone to have some wish for self expression. Never be afraid of beginning. Think of painting as an adventure. You know what you are looking for, and will discover all kinds of unexpected things on the way, not only about painting, but about the world and yourself. If the most ordinary attempts at painting lead us to a greater knowledge of the universe, then it is worth while. One might, once in a lifetime, do one marvellous little painting to which people will always respond. We are all familiar with this in anonymous poems in anthologies, and hymn-tunes of classic grandeur by quite forgotten composers.

Beginning to paint is about three things, more or less, being brave and actually starting. Then getting to know your equipment, paints, boards and brushes. Once you have even the vaguest idea what you want to do, you will be painting. For anyone painting, of beginner or otherwise, regular work is essential. So is a special place for working; if you cannot manage a whole room, then just a corner, where you can always have your equipment to hand.

Writers and musicians of all kinds say that regular hours are a basic principle of their working method. The same should be so with painters. The idea of an artist working to 'inspiration', is a pure fantasy, and of no painter anyone has heard about is it true! Even if one is not in the mood at any time to paint, but one starts despite this, the mood to paint will come of itself. Never worry about painting going wrong. It will go wrong sometimes, but it will go right too. Often enough, the times when painting has gone badly are times when you have probably learned more than you think. Of course, this book cannot be about making painting easy – then it would not be worth doing – but it is an attempt to remove the worst difficulties. Rules are kept to a minimum, or in some cases several rules are suggested. In any case, there is only one abiding rule – to do a good painting.

Much of the information given is related to discussions and questions that beginners have asked at art clubs and societies. Everyone one met there were painting for thoroughly worthwhile reasons: response to beauty and colour, and the wish to give somebody else pleasure. This is where the beginner can teach the established artist rather than the other way about. When one visits the most up-to-date contemporary galleries, public and private, it is obvious that there is a serious crisis in official art. Much of the work that is receiving acclaim, and money, appears to be an entirely private expression of the artist, with no wish to communicate with the ordinary person. There is now open breach between the artist and his public. One can ask in vain, who is this for? Why was this painted? If the human and normal values of art are to be preserved, it may be that the people painting for pure pleasure may preserve them. Or it may be something deeper than just pleasure, preserving in paint a moment of intense emotion, or attempting to give permanent form to something we believe to be noble and moving.

Oil painting was developed in Flanders in the early fifteenth century. The pretty legend that it was developed by the Van Eyck brothers is now discredited by art historians. Previous to the discovery that colours could be ground in oil, colour was ground in egg yellow, tempora, or paint was applied direct on to wet lime plaster, alfresco. Oil paint, unlike these other paints, is slow drying, the surface can be worked into, and paint can be built up, smudged and blurred. Leonardo da Vinci's discovery that a blurred edge in oil paint had an ambiguous interpretation, totally altered the history of art.

Each chapter will end with a book list, and a list, where it is relevant, of paintings to look at.

Here is a list of other popular and excellent books on oil painting for beginners:

A Stepladder to Painting by Jan Gordon, revised by Colin Hayes. Faber and Faber.

Starting to Paint in Oils by John Raynes. Studio Vista.

Thames and Hudson publish art books on every artist period of art history and culture, and famous museums. These publications by Thames and Hudson cannot be sufficiently praised.

Phaidon Press also are famous publishers of beautifully produced and scholarly art books.

Introducing Oil Painting, by Michael Pope. Batsford.

The Technique of Oil Painting by Colin Hayes. Batsford.

It is worth reading as many books as you can on how to paint, as each one will tell you something new. Naturally, you will find contradictions from one book to another; when you get to know your paint and board thoroughly, you will make up your own mind. It is barely possible for a writer on painting to be truly detached. Personal preferences are inevitable. Neither, of course, can the book list be comprehensive. It is only intended to start you off finding books of all kinds to inspire your work. Not only art books, but every other kind.

CHAPTER TWO

BASIC EQUIPMENT

Painting will mean expense. This chapter is not about avoiding this, but it is about spending wisely. It is tempting in art shops to get carried away by gadgets that look amusing enough, but one never uses them.

Collect empty jars and tins for your oil and turpentine, never plastic, as oil and turpentine rot plastic containers. Collect also cotton and linen rags – you will use a lot of these, though never use nylon or wool rags.

Every artist colourman sells splendid, ready-fitted-out boxes for painting in oils. But if you want to save money, keep your paints in tin boxes. Store brushes in jars in the studio, and carry brushes about wrapped up in clean rag. Beach bags are excellent for taking your paint equipment about with you.

Take care in choosing an easel. A flimsy one with screws that get stuck, and falls down at the least thing, is worse than useless. Many painters to name Bonnard, Klee, and Jackson Pollock, never used one at all. The great advantage of an easel is to be able to stand back from your painting while, at the same time, comparing the picture to the thing you are painting. It is always as well to keep a look-out for the fine old fashioned studio easels, now not made, but they turn up in junk shops some times. The most popular easel is the radial (Fig. 1).

What one paints on is called the 'support' – at least this is what it is called in all the advanced books on techniques, though for convenience in later chapters I shall refer to the canvas or board as the 'board'. Your equipment and methods are an essential part of how you express yourself, and no aspect of materials should be treated casually. This does not

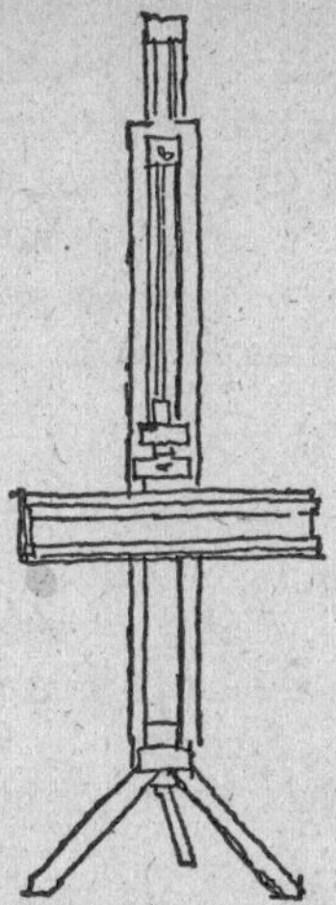

Fig. 1 Radial easel.

however, mean you should make unnecessary complications where they can be avoided.

All art suppliers sell ready-made patented boards, and prepared papers for oil painting. The latter are inclined to have a rather slippery surface.

Here then is a list of supports ordinarily obtainable:

CANVAS. The traditional support for oil painting. You can buy it ready primed and on stretchers. Admittedly, this is the most expensive support you can use. Or, slightly cheaper, buy rolls of ready-made primed canvas and fix it to your own stretchers. Canvas is marvellous to use. It has a drum-like surface, that has in itself a receptiveness to the touch of a paint brush. Canvas can also be bought plain, and you size and prime it yourself. One does see cotton and jute used instead of true linen; these are impermanent, and should be avoided unless you are deliberately painting something not intended to last.

WOOD PANELS. These are also traditional. They are inclined to warp and split. Probably not worth the trouble.

PLYWOOD. Due to method of manufacture inclined to warp and curl, so not worth the trouble.

GLASS AND METALS. Have been used in the past, but for obvious reasons neither can be recommended.

CARDBOARD. Is likely to grow fungus and bacteria. None-the-less it has been used by many painters who like the warm brown colour as a middle tone for oil sketching. Use cardboard if you do not mind overmuch about permanence. Size both sides.

PAPER. Stout brown paper has been used for oil sketching for the same reason as cardboard, the warm colour being agreeable. More permanent than cardboard, it can be primed as well as sized. Sizing is essential.

HARDBOARD. This is the most permanent support for oil painting, and the most favoured by experts on technique. It has the advantage that, if a painting would be improved by cutting a bit off, or you want to paint on an unusually shaped support, there is no difficulty in sawing hardboard to any shape you please. The grained side of hardboard should never be used; it is essential to use the smooth side. This should be sandpapered slightly before applying size and priming. Hardboard is very easily obtainable.

SUNDEALA. This is a kind of hardboard that many painters prefer. It has the advantage of coming in various thicknesses, and a large painting on a thick enough piece of Sundeala does not need any supports at the back. Sundeala has a very agreeable soft surface, which should be sized and primed. Sundeala is not quite as readily available as hardboard, and you may have to order whole panels at once.

TERYLENE. A point that may lead to controversy, but some technicians believe that Terylene on stretchers, primed direct with acrylic priming is the support in the future. There can certainly be no harm in experimenting.

SIZE

SIZE is weak glue. When you are using any ground that contains oil, sizing is essential, as it stops the oil corroding the support, which will occur if there are not a couple of

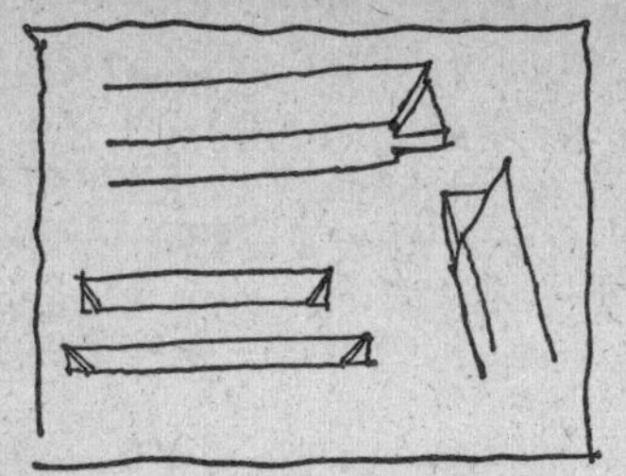

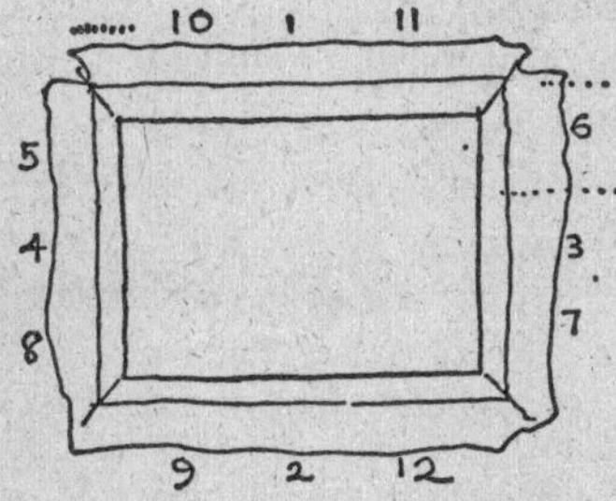

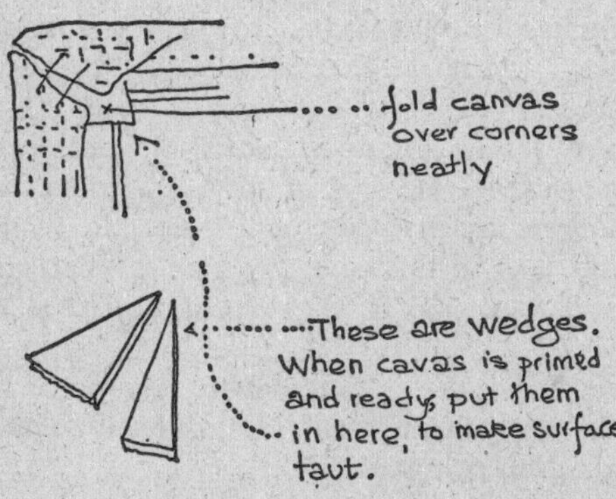

Fig. 2 Sizing unprimed canvas.

coats of size. The old fashioned skin glues, usually rabbit-skin glue, has never been bettered. You should use one part of glue to fifteen parts of water. Let it soak. Then heat but do not let it boil. Use size when it is warm. It saves considerable time and trouble to size many boards at the same time. Boards should be sized both sides.

Sizing unprimed canvas is a bit more complicated – the method is illustrated in Fig. 2.

Be warned, never stretch unsized canvas too tight, as when the canvas dries out it will shrink. Too tight stretching can lead to the stretchers warping.

If you are using one of the new acrylic emulsion primers, you need not size the support at all.

Prime your support if it is to have any degree of permanence.

Winsor and Newton market a very good size specially prepared for artists.

PRIMING

To give your support any degree of permanence it must be primed. The most up-to-date primers are acrylic based. Both Rowney & Co. and Winsor and Newton market very good ones, which are the results of very careful research. Acrylic priming has the advantage of being very convenient. It needs no sizing, and it can be used on any of the supports mentioned above. If you really want to save money you can use a very good quality emulsion paint on your support. Always give more than one coat of acrylic primers. I have heard some painters say that they find an acrylic priming a bit dead to work on; in this case you may wish to try the older traditional methods. A very popular primer is the following . . .

EGG EMULSION PRIMING. Ingredients: Egg (one large) which is also the unit of measurement, linseed oil, Titanium white powder, rabbit skin size.

Method: Break the whole egg into a screw top jar. Shake egg up thoroughly.

Add to the egg in jar equal quantity of linseed oil, shake

again very thoroughly. Now add water equal to the amount of egg and oil and shake again vigorously. Make quite sure the mixture is thoroughly emulsified.

On a glass slab mix this emulsion with the titanium white powder to make a smooth stiff paste. Use a palette knife for mixing. Now thin the paste with the size to the consistency of house paint. The method of preparing size is given on page 12. Obviously to increase quantities double the amounts given above.

EGG EMULSION PRIMER. This can be used on any support which has been sized. It is very satisfying to prepare one's own priming. It also has the advantage that you can add any dry powder colour of your choosing if you like the idea of working on a tinted ground.

You could also add pumice powder for a surface with a 'tooth' to it.

WHITE LEAD GROUND. Also a traditional ground. Heavier than the other, but a very attractive surface to work. If you are buying it ready-made you should be sure that it contains linseed oil. Use two or three coats. Whether you are using ready-made lead-based ground, or are preparing your own, you must take care. Lead is very poisonous, and it should not be inhaled, or allowed to get into cuts. Wash thoroughly after handling. White lead ground is flexible so most suitable for canvas. The proportions for mixing your own are:

Three parts of lead carbonate to one part of linseed oil. Mix with a palette knife on a slab, and thin with turpentine (genuine, not white spirit). You should leave a bit more than a week after each coat of priming, and give two or three coats. Leave for another week before painting.

To sum up then, about supports and primings (or grounds): a choice of support finally depends on your response to different surfaces. Experiment at first with as many as you can. You may find them all agreeable, or you may find that one particular type suits you the best. The fact of preparing your own grounds etc., apart from saving money, is part of the physical response to your materials.

MEDIUMS

These are what you use with your paint to thin or thicken it when you are painting.

GENUINE GUM TURPENTINE is the basic thinner for oil paint. It can be used alone as a thinner for oil paint, or for perhaps the first coat; but turpentine alone makes the surface of the painting very delicate, and so it cannot be entirely recommended.

White Spirit, sometimes marketed as Turpentine substitute should not be used for oil painting at all, use only for cleaning brushes.

LINSEED OIL. Of all the mediums and drying oils, this is most generally used, being the most suitable and convenient. It should be used with turpentine, in proportion of two parts of turpentine to one of linseed oil. Always rinse brushes thoroughly after use, as linseed oil rots the hairs and bristles. There are other oils but linseed is quite the best.

THICKENING OIL PAINT. If the idea is to use oil paint freely yet thickly, you can use the synthetic resin gels supplied by both Winsor and Newton and Rowney. They are convenient, reliable and quick drying. They can, in fact, be used thin as well, and are also very convenient to take on holiday, as they come prepared in tubes. But if you want a really thick medium that you can thoroughly enjoy applying with palette knife (more about this later), here is a traditional recipe. All materials obtainable at art stores:

Damar Varnish – Four parts
Beeswax – Two parts
Turpentine – One part

Heat the ingredients in a double boiler till the wax has dissolved. Remove from the heater and stir while cooling.

While you are working, keep two tins at your side. One of the medium, and the other of turpentine to rinse your brushes. After twenty-four hours or so the sediment will sink to the bottom of the tin, then you can pour off the clear liquid into another tin. This is quite a saving. (see Fig. 3).

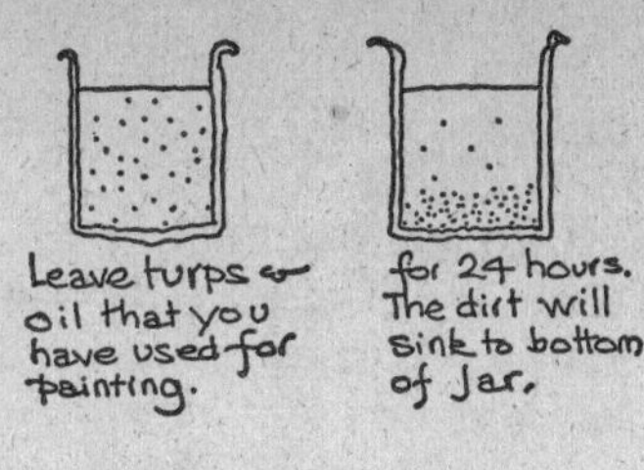

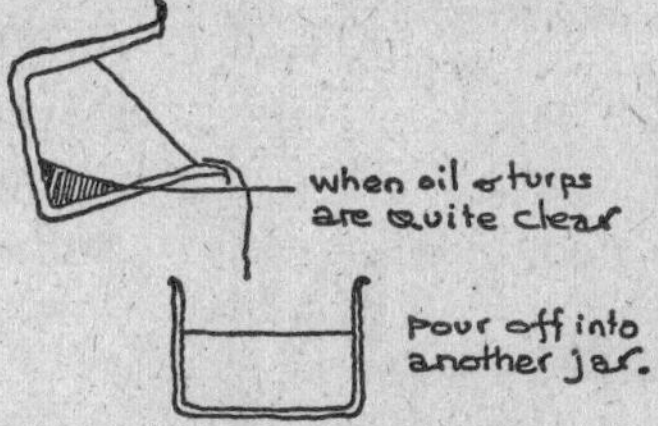

Fig. 3 A useful saving.

PALETTES

These are what one lays one's colours out on, and on which one mixes them. We are all familiar with the traditional artist's palettes from numerous self portraits. These

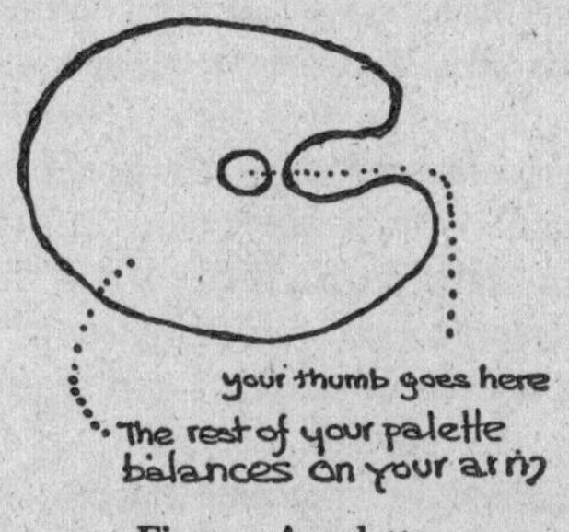

Fig. 4 A palette.

are usually of mahogany, or teak, and the idea is that you hold it in your hand balanced on your arm, while you paint. Many painters enjoy the feel of the natural quality of the wood. Care of a wooden palette is essential. After use it

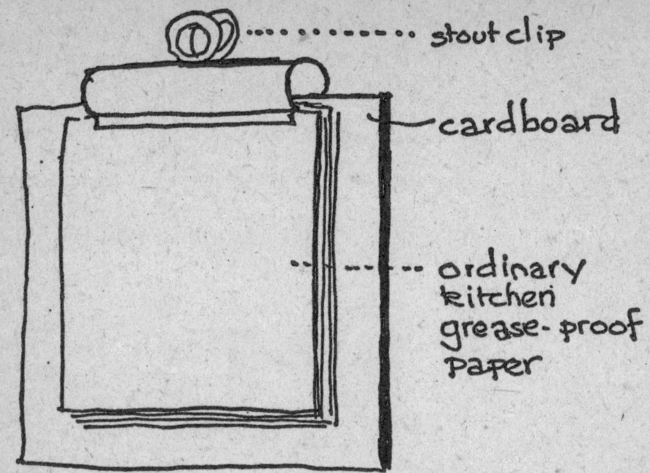

Fig. 5 Making a disposable palette.

should be scraped quite clean with a palette knife, and then you should rub in linseed oil to preserve the surface of the wood. In time a wooden palette developes a fine patina.

If you find that holding a palette is uncomfortable, the following surfaces rested on a stool or table are perfectly suitable:

Thick glass, white laminated plastic like Formica, and china slabs all make perfectly suitable surfaces to mix paint. Some painters prefer the white surface of plastic to the brown of a palette, as it is easier to mix colour. Also, plastic can be cut into any shape you please, useful if you want to experiment with a colour wheel (see Chapter 4).

Paint can be left on the edge of a palette if it is clean after a session of work, and should remain workable for about two days. If you are leaving it longer, then cover with grease-proof paper.

Disposable palettes for travelling are sold in art shops. To save money here is how you make your own. All you need is cardboard, greaseproof paper and a stout clip (see Fig. 5).

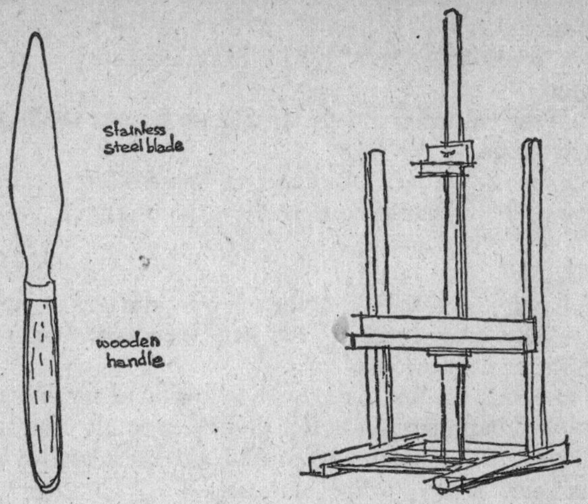

Fig. 6 Palette knife. Fig. 7 Large studio easel.

PALETTE KNIFE

Get a medium sized one. Use for cleaning your palette, and for mixing your own primings. And of course for painting. More about this in the next chapter.

Other pieces of equipment that are useful but not basic essentials are a stapling gun – for tacking down canvas, and pinning-up drawings – and a double glue boiler.

One must be comfortable to concentrate on painting. If it is tiring for you to stand, then do not ever feel you must. It will not be any better for your work. The same is true of holding a palette in your hand the whole time.

SOME RECOMMENDED BOOKS

Very convenient and useful is:

Materials and Methods Of Painting by Lynton Lamb. Oxford Paperbacks.

The following books are more advanced but give exhaustive accounts of media, supports, varnishes, colour, etc.:

The Artist's Handbook of Materials and Techniques by Ralph Meyer. Faber and Faber.

The Materials of the Artist by Max Doerner; 1949. Hart Davies.

Painting Materials by Gettens and Stout, 1966. Dover Publications.

(Dover Paperback publications are a New York firm, but their books can be ordered in this country.)

TAILPIECE

I have just discovered that big studio easels are still manufactured in France. They can be ordered from a large Art Store; at a price.

Somebody has just told me the following recipe. When you size hardboard, stretch butter muslin smoothly over surface while the size is wet. The muslin will stick to the board. When size is dry, prime as usual. You will then have a canvas-type painting surface. Many people find this support very satisfactory.

CHAPTER THREE

BRUSHES AND PAINTING KNIVES

The feel of paint brushed never fails to thrill a painter. The white, rough hog hair brushes, and the sleek springy sable become beloved and exciting objects to any painter. Hog hair and sable are the oil painter's brushes. Never be tempted to get cheap brushes; it is a poor economy, a continual frustration. What you have to express as a painter is never above your materials, it is an integral part of them. So always get the very best brushes. With care, they last a very long time.

Fig. 8 shows the shapes of brushes available.

To begin with, obtain two sables. Sable is the most celebrated of all animal furs. It is strong, resilient, and always keeps its shape. Some paint brushes are made of kolinsky sable. This is good but does not have the quality of true sable. By general consent most artists use sable brushes for preliminary drawing, and for fine detail. This is because a sable brush lays on paint so smoothly you do not see individual brush strokes at all. It is likely that the early Flemish painters used only sable brushes. There is no reason why one should not use sable only, if the way they respond to you and the paint, is what you like.

Hog hair brushes are tougher than sable. To begin with, get two large ones of any shape, four in the medium range of any shape that appeals to you, and one small brush. Paint brushes are as individual as paint nibs. What are ideal for some are wrong for others, and your brushes, like a nib, take on something of you. In photographs of artist's studios one sees them with jars and jars of brushes. Ideally, if one can afford it, one should have many brushes, keeping some for each range of colour.

If there are rules one cannot avoid in painting, the care of

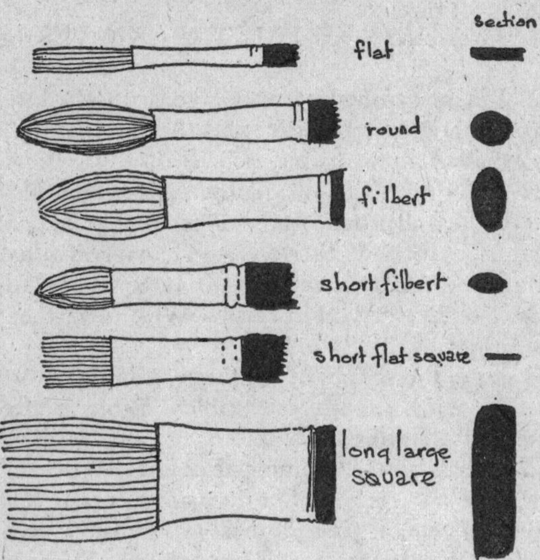

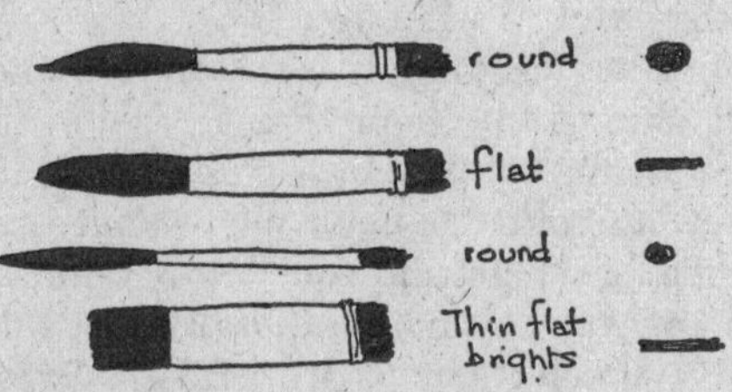

Fig. 8 Brushes.

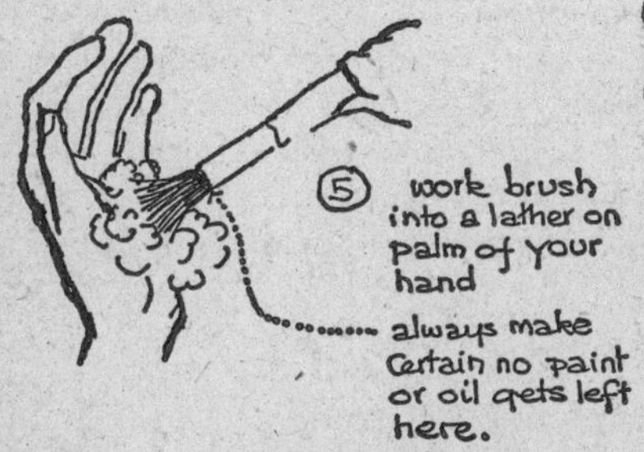

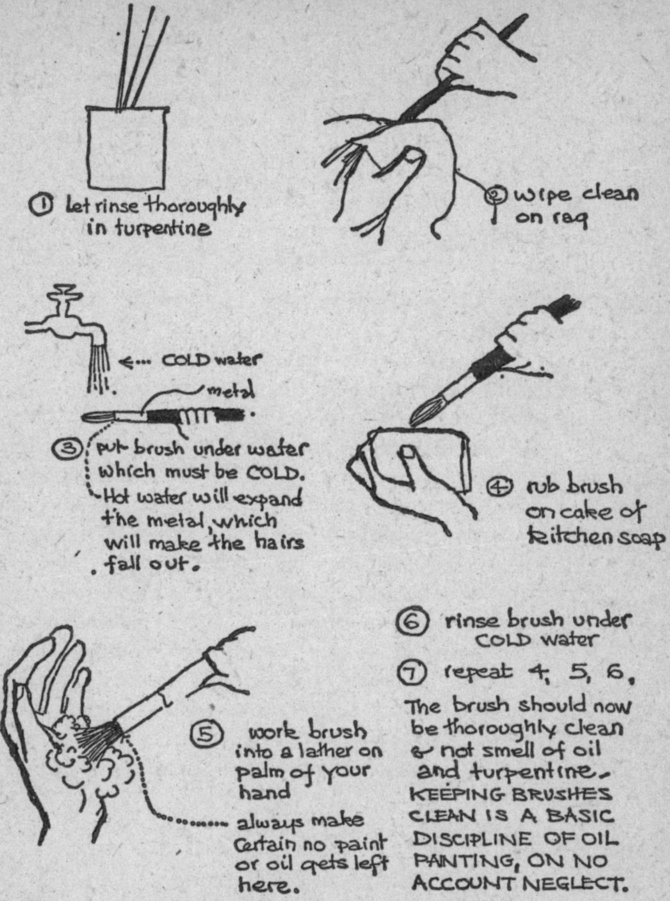

Fig. 9 How to wash your brushes.

brushes is certainly one of them. Not only does it save money, it is a basic and essential part of the respect for one's materials. Wash brushes after every painting session with kitchen soap, and cold water. Not warm water, as it expands the metal part of the brush and thereby shortens its life.

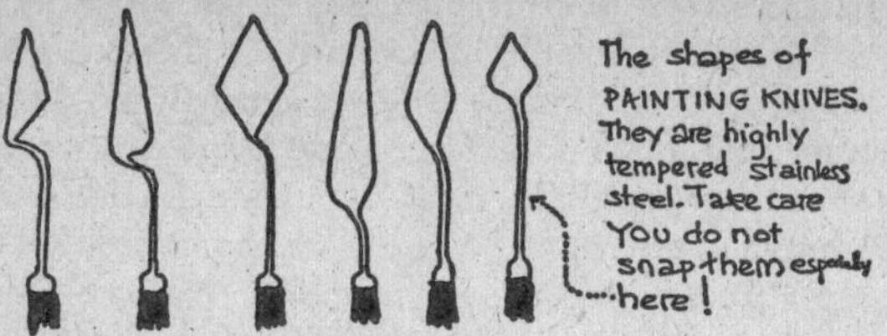

Fig. 10 Painting knives.

As you paint, you will get to know the brushes that suit your own way best.

Paint can be put on, and for that matter equally effectively taken off, with a palette knife. Palette knives become very finely tempered with use. You can smooth paint out with them on your board to make rather an unusual surface to paint on. If you become addicted to the agreeable sensation (and it is agreeable and expressive), of painting with a palette knife, then you could try painting knives. They are made specially for this purpose. Unlike the ordinary palette knife they are hand ground and highly tempered. Both palette knives and painting knives – like brushes, have to be kept clean, and paint should not be allowed to harden on them. If you are mixing paint with pumice powder or sand to get unusual textures, it might be as well to apply the paint with a knife. Sand and pumice wear out brushes in no time. Old, worn-down brushes can be still useful for drawing in a painting.

ROOMS AND LIGHT

One seldom has much choice over the room one works in, and is obliged to make do with what is available. But if there is any element of choice, the light should be clear and even. By tradition this is a north light. A net curtain diffuses light, which is useful if you have to work in a changing light.

DAY OR ARTIFICIAL LIGHT

Daylight is quite the optimum to work in, as it has a vast range, and therefore a greater number of pigments reflect back their colours than is the case in artificial light. If you look at any artificial light through a refraction grid, the spectrum you will see has gaps of various colours which are all there by daylight. For all that, some painters are perfectly happy to work by artificial light. If you work with a limited palette, or with a palette biased to earth colours, artificial light probably will not make much difference. One can otherwise use the working time by artificial light usefully enough to work on one's drawings.

CHAPTER FOUR

PAINT AND COLOUR

Until about eighty years ago, some very great artists believed that colour was a mere addition to the noble and higher concepts of drawing and composition. However, as more and more scientific research was done into optics and light, the idea that colour in itself had no appeal to the mind, no longer appeared to be true. It used to be believed that colour only appealed to the senses, and not the mind. This may be so, but how can one decide where the senses and the mind divide? It is certainly true looking at the history of Western art that some painters are natural colourists while others respond more to light and shade, or the drawn line. The nineteenth century saw the most fascinating researches into the analysis of colour and light in the representation of nature. In the early twentieth century the idea grew of colour being used for its psychological effect. It may be that colour in itself, or in nature, may have been the first thing that attracted us to painting, and this is a perfectly good starting point.

Probably, if you have looked at other handbooks on beginning painting, each one will give a set of colours with which to start painting. Each book's list will be different. This is unavoidable, as it is in the end up to you to discover your own palette. In any art shop, or painting materials catalogue, you will see oil paints listed as Students' Colours and Artists' Colours. Students' Colours are made with the deliberate policy of keeping costs as low as possible. Oil colours should be pure pigment ground in linseed oil – which is how Artists' Colours are made. Some pigments made of rare metallic oxides are very expensive. Therefore Students' Colours use dyes that imitate these very expensive colours. In the cheaper colours, there are additives in

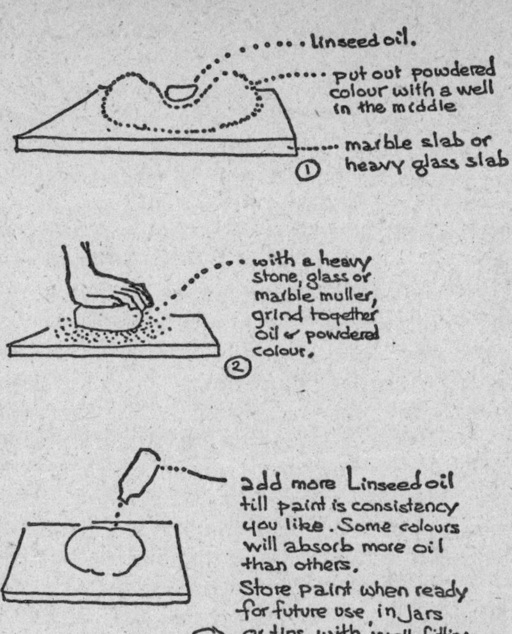

Fig. 11 Grinding your own colours.

Students' Colours. The advantage of Students' Colours is that they are cheap, and at all times entirely permanent. Untiring research goes into their production. I admit to a complete bias to Artists' Colours, for their clarity, intensity and refinement. A perfectly reasonable compromise, however, is to use Students' Colours in white, yellow ochre, blacks and browns. Devoted and patient research goes into the making of Artists' Colours; there is every reason to take full advantage of all this, and to use some of the new and delightful colours that have come into use over the last twenty years or so. A reasonably comprehensive list of Artists' Colours is given on pages 29-35. Every one of them is permanent. Colours are graded according to durability, starting at four star down to one. No colour less than three stars is listed here.

This may disagree violently with many opinions, but true greens, oranges, and purples cannot be mixed effectively in oil paint. Theoretically, in colours of light, blue, red and yellow can be mixed to make green, purple and orange, but this really does not work in paint, and you get rather dingy imitations of the true colour. The suggestions for a palette to begin will include orange, green and purple. Obviously, if you would rather not use any particular colour, either leave it out or choose something else. A perfectly good way of choosing colours for your palette, is to have what takes your fancy, providing it does not interact badly on the other colours – which no colour will do providing you stick to the three or four star colours, or the ones marked 'selected'. There is not much point in using impermanent colours.

So far nothing has been said about grinding one's own colours. This can be and is done by painters, but is only cheaper on a very large scale, and seems worth the trouble only if you have plenty of spare time. One of the main disadvantages is actually obtaining enough dry powdered pigment, unless you live in a large city. For all that, Fig. 11 shows how it is done . . .

BASIC OBSERVATIONS ABOUT OIL PAINT

The inclination of most oil colours is to be transparent or semi-transparent until you add white, which makes them opaque. It is possible to paint entirely in layers of transparent colour. The addition of white to any colour quite alters its character. In the lists of colour given, they are classified according to basic chemical content, tone, covering power (listed as density), degree of transparency, and general remarks.

YELLOWS

COLOUR	CONTENT	TONE	DENSITY	TRANSPARENCY	GENERAL REMARKS
Winsor Lemon (Rowney market the same colour as 'Lemon Yellow')	Synthetic dye	The lightest toned oil colour next to white.	Medium	Semi-trans.	An indispensable colour. Clear, pungent, nearest in pigment to spectrum yellow. Other colours can be mixed with it to make a variety of colours.
Cadmium Lemon	Cadmium Sulphide and Cadmium Selenide	See above	Medium	Semi-trans.	A refined and beautiful lemon. As it is very expensive the above colour is as good.
Winsor Yellow	Synthetic dye	Very light	Medium	Semi-trans.	Not essential in your palette unless you like it. A touch of red added to lemon yellows has the same effect.
Cadmium Yellow	Cadmium sulphide and Cadmium Selenide	Light	Strong	Semi-trans.	A fine yellow, but expensive.
Cadmium Orange	Cadmium Sulphide and Cadmium Selenide	Medium	Strong	Semi-opaque	A beautiful, clear, strong orange. The best. Expensive but goes a long way.
Winsor Orange	Synthetic dye	Medium	Medium	Semi-trans.	A reasonable alternative to Cadmium Orange.

This table has not included Chrome Yellows and Oranges. If permamence is really of no importance, they could be used, but are not recommended.

REDS – ALL PERMANENT

COLOUR	CONTENT	TONE	DENSITY	TRANSPARENCY	GENERAL REMARKS
Cadmium Scarlet	Cadmium Sulpho-Selenide	Light	Strong	Semi-trans.	A very bright red, nearly orange.
Cadmium Red	Sulpho-Selenide	Medium	Strong	Semi-trans.	A true red, nearest to Spectrum red.
Rowney Red	Organic dye	Medium	Strong	Semi-trans.	A good bright red an alternative to Cadmium Red, as it is less expensive.
Winsor Red	Organic dye	Medium	Strong	Semi-trans.	A good bright red an alternative to Cadmium Red, as it is less expensive.
Rose Doré or Winsor & Newton Rose Madder	Dye Dye	Light Light	Very weak	Entirely trans. Entirely trans.	Beautiful, clear for glazing dainty flesh tints. Gets lost when mixed.
Crimson Alizarin	Synthetic dye	Dark	Medium	Transparent	A cold dark red. Useful for glazing. Inclines slightly to brown in mixtures. Many painters find it indispensable.
Rowney Rose (Winsor & Newton call it Permanent Rose)	Quinacridone	Dark	Medium	Entirely trans.	A variant of Crimson, veers to blue. Does not lose its character on being mixed. Mixes with white to very true, pretty pinks.

PURPLES – ALL PERMANENT

COLOUR	CONTENT	TONE	DENSITY	TRANSPARENCY	GENERAL REMARKS
Cobalt Violet	Cobalt salts, some poisonous	The lightest toned purple there is	Weak	Semi-trans.	A beautiful warm violet much favoured by the Impressionists and the post-Impressionists.
Permanent Magenta	Quinacridone	Dark	Strong	Entirely trans. Changed drastically by addition of white	A new colour, very bright clear unusual and cold. A very good glazing colour.
Rowney Permanent Mauve and Winsor Violet	Synthetic dye	Very dark	Strong	Quite trans.	Make unusual and interesting combinations with other colours. Useful in some cases as a darkener. Neutral neither warm nor cold.

BLUES – ALL PERMANENT

COLOUR	CONTENT	TONE	DENSITY	TRANSPARENCY	GENERAL REMARKS
Cerulian	Cobalt based	Lightest of all the blues. Unusual and useful for that reason.	Strong	Entirely opaque	A very useful colour, mixes to make delightful neutral colours. In colour biased toward green.
Manganese	Manganese	Fairly light	Medium	Entirely trans.	Similar to above, but greener; the nearest in oil paint to a turquoise blue.
Cobalt	Cobalt based	Of the blues the middle toned one	Strong	Semi-opaque	A bright and excellent colour, clear and strong. Much favoured by the post-Impressionists.
Ultramarine	A chemical imitation of the expensive Lapiz lazuli of the old masters	Dark	Strong	Transparent	The traditional blue, and used by every oil painter. Beautiful, clear and the 'bluest' of the blues. Indispensable, as it is nearest you can get in pigment to spectrum blue.
Winsor Blue (Monastial Blue is Rowney's name for the same colour)	Phthalocyanine synthetic dye	Dark	Strong	Entirely trans. Character of these blues changes completely when white is added, and they become quite opaque	Greenish dark blues. Useful as darkeners. Make good glazes, they mix to make unusual and interesting colours.
Indigo	Synthetic dye	The darkest toned of all the blues	Strong	As above	In colour neutral, rather like blue-black ink. Useful as a darkener. A gentle colour not too self-assertive.

GREENS – ALL PERMANENT

COLOUR	CONTENT	TONE	DENSITY	TRANSPARENCY	GENERAL REMARKS
Cadmium Green light	Cadmium Lemon and viridian	The lightest green there is	Medium	Semi-opaque	A very brilliant green, exciting, but use with care. Makes unusual mixtures, a warm green. Yellowish.
Rowney or Winsor Emerald	Synthetic dye	This is another light green	Medium	Semi-opaque	A cold light colour can be made warm. Bright and good in mixing.
Terra Vert	Natural earth	Light	Weakest of all the permanent colours	Transparent, turns white to a delicate grey	A beautiful but very delicate green. Warm.
Viridian	Chromium hydroxide hydrated	Dark	Medium	Transparent	Probably the most popular of the greens. Mixes excellently with other colours to make many variations of greens. A cold colour, with shades of blue.

NATURAL EARTHS, NEUTRALS, BROWNS

COLOUR	CONTENT	TONE	DENSITY	TRANSPARENCY	GENERAL REMARKS
Yellow Ochre	Natural earth	Lightest of earth colours	Strong	Opaque. Makes colours it mixes with opaque	An indispensable colour, mixes excellently.
Flesh Colour (Winsor and Newton)	Mixture containing flake white	Light	Medium	Dense opaque	A neutral in an agreeable terra cotta colour. As much used in landscape as flesh. Not an essential.
Light Red	Calcined yellow ochre, therefore a natural earth	Medium	Strong	Semi-opaque	Another indispensable colour, mixes excellently.
Raw Umber	Natural earth	Dark	Medium	The only really transparent natural earth. Changes to dense opacity when mixed with white, to an almost mauve shade	A neutral brown with a distinctly green shade. Very popular with most artists, as it mixes well, and is particularly useful for laying in the beginning of a painting.
Burnt Umber	Natural earth	Dark	Medium	Semi-opaque	A true brown.
Venetian Red	Iron oxide	Medium	Strong	Semi-opaque	A very strong neutral red. Use with great care, as it can drown other colours. Slightly more crimson than light red.
Sepia (Rowney)	Synthetic organic dye, on an inert base	Very dark	Medium	Transparent	An agreeable brown with hint of purple.

WHITES AND BLACKS

COLOUR	CONTENT	TONE	DENSITY	TRANSPARENCY	GENERAL REMARKS
Flake White	Lead Carbonate	The lightest colour on your palette	Strong, thick, heavy	Opaque. Makes all colours you mix it with opaque too	The white of all the oil painters of the past. Good if you like working into thick paint.
Zinc White	Zinc Oxide	The lightest colour on your palette	Weak	Most transparent of the whites	Brittle and slow drying.
Titanium White	Titanium Dioxide	If possible lighter than the other whites	Medium	Medium	Very white and clear, good for scumbling.
Lamp Black Ivory Black	Carbon Carbon	Darkest colour on the palette	Medium Medium	Opaque Opaque	Black is a very drastic darkener. Take care it does not make the colours cold and heavy. Black goes rather dull when there are large areas of it, and the colour dries. Many painters will not use black.

Here is a recommended list of colours to start with. When you have got to know these you could add more or change them for other ones of your choice:

White (any)
Lemon Yellow
Yellow Ochre
Orange (Cadmium or Winsor)
Cadmium or Winsor Red
Crimson Alizarin or Rose (Rowney or Permanent)
Cobalt Violet or Permanent Mauve
Ultramarine Blue
Cobalt Blue or Cerulean Blue
Viridian Green
Raw Umber
Light Red

ARRANGING YOUR PALETTE

There are several ways of setting out colours on your palette – or you might even invent your own system. But you should have some sort of system and not put colours out anyhow. It is always better to put out a bit too much colour rather than too little; meanness with colour is no saving.

The scientific theory that has most directly affected painters is that of complementary colours. Probably, you are familiar with it already, but as it is exceedingly useful it is worth repeating.

In white light there are three primary colours.

Red, blue and yellow green.
Red + blue combine to make purple, leaving yellow-green
Yellow + red combine to make orange, leaving blue
Blue + yellow combine to make green, leaving red.

So, yellow and purple, etc., are said to be complementary to each other. You can prove this by looking intensely at a patch of red. If you then look at a white area it appears

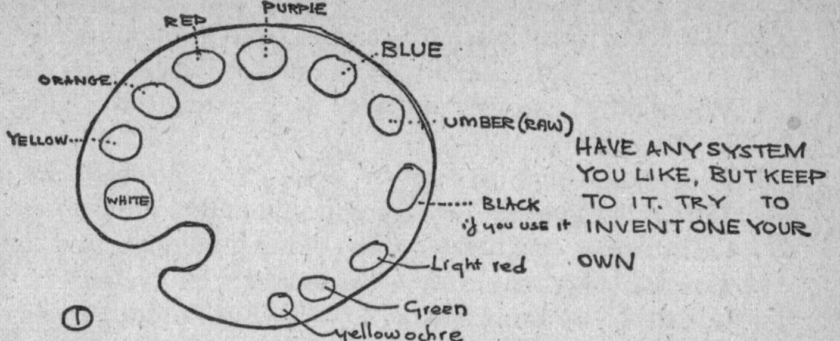

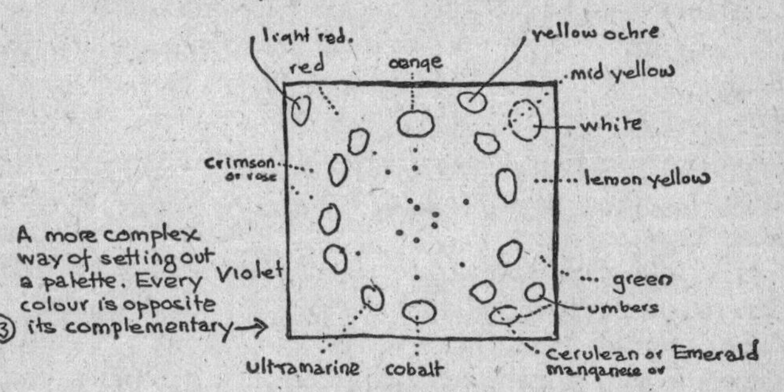

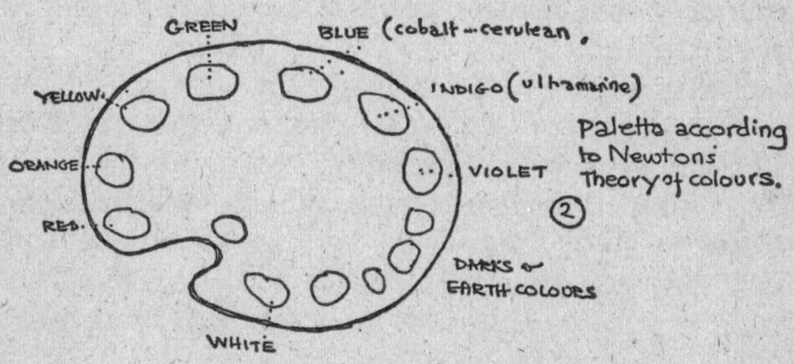

Fig. 12 Arranging your palette.

distinctly greenish. In painting, blue can be made to look the more vivid by putting it next to orange. An entirely neutral grey will take on shades of the opposite colour of any colour it is next to. As explained earlier, however, you do not get effective oranges, purples and greens by mixing primaries.

Van Gogh, Gauguin, and the founder of abstract art, Kandinsky, used colour for its emotional and psychological effect. There is every reason why colour should be used in this way. To many people certain colours are associated with special emotions, and this is so in whole cultures and peoples. We are all familiar with the symbolic purples and blacks of Lent. Some painters use a lot of brown, as though to give their subject matter greater seriousness. Kandinsky even equated his colours with notes of music.

Goethe had a theory of colours that Turner found inspiring.

SOME FURTHER READING ABOUT COLOUR

Colour: Basic Principles and New Directions by Patricia Sloane. Studio Vista.

The Art of Colour by Itten. Reinhold, New York.

History of Colour In Painting by Faber Birren. Reinhold, New York.

Colour For the Artist by Hans Schwarz. Studio Vista.

TAILPIECE

The French scientist Chevreuil wrote an absorbing and influential treatise on colour in the last century. It is still worthy of study, though copies are difficult to find. There is a translation into English. A very good library could probably get you one.

Some quotations

Van Gogh wrote to his brother Theo: 'Red and Green, the terrible colours of men's passions.'

Gauguin wrote: 'Colour which is vibration the same as

music is, it reaches to what is most general and therefore vaguest in nature – its interior force.'

Delacroix: 'Colour is the probity of art.' His great rival Ingres had solemnly announced that 'drawing is the probity of art.' They are both right!

CHAPTER FIVE

YOUR FIRST PAINTING

To begin, you should set out your equipment and put out the colours on your palette. This will help clarify your thoughts and establish the mood for painting.

For your first painting you could try an abstract, though if the idea is too daunting, go on to the next chapter. However, if the idea of putting colour and paint on boards inspired you to paint in the first place, this is as good a starting point as any other. One hears the commonplace remark that one 'has to be able to draw before one can paint abstracts'. This has no foundation in fact. An eye for shape and colour is quite enough. Not that painting abstracts is an easy way out; the difficulties are of a different kind.

At the beginning of any painting, the white of a board surface looks formidable. So instead of putting off beginning – which is all too easy to do – be brave and start to paint directly on to your board. Without any preliminary drawing. Later, there will be times when you will have to do a variety of preliminary drawings, but not now. The idea of starting with an abstract is so that you will start to get to know the character and feel of oil paint.

Take any colour of your choosing. For example, ultramarine. Mix some in the centre of your palette with your turpentine and linseed oil. You will now see that oil paint can be as transparent as water colour. At all times you should start by using thin paint, working up thicker as you go, if you want your painting to be in any way permanent.

With the colour of your choosing, paint a shape on your board, any shape.

The paint will be quite thin on your board. Now what to do next? This painting is a sort of exploration, not knowing quite what you will find on arrival at the end, though you will discover a lot on the way. You could make the whole painting variations on the colour that you started with. See how light you can get a colour by mixing with turpentine and oil. Or by mixing with white. White is the usual lightener of oil paint. It also makes the colour quite opaque. Then darken the original colour. Try using any colour other than black, which is a very drastic darkener. Stand back from the painting every so often and look at it carefully. Are the shapes working together? Are the tones too even? By tones it is generally taken to mean the equivalents in black and white and shades of grey of each colour; like one would get from taking a photograph of a painting. A very useful experiment is attempting to lighten colours without white, and darkening without black.

Another experiment in abstraction is using opposite colours. Start with one colour direct from the tube, not mixing with any colour. For example, an area of yellow, clearly on your board. Surround it with white which has the merest tint of raw umber. It will take on an unmistakable mauvish colour. (You could of course do the same with any other colour, blue, red, etc.)

Yet the background can lose its mauvish character by adding yellow to the colour. A colour, then, can be quite neutralised by adding to it its opposite. This is very useful if you want a sort of half colour but not exactly a shadow. The background is now a rather indifferent colour. Add some purple, and you will see how you cannot add a colour to a painting without it affecting all the other colours. With such obviously contrasting colours tonally, the size of each area of colour is important. Experiment on the surface of the board – is a large area of yellow more powerful than a small area of purple? Or does a large area of purple kill a smaller area of yellow or intensify it? Experiment for yourself and form your own conclusions (Fig. 14). Stand back again. Perhaps there is an agreeable effect that has happened by apparent accident. This often occurs in a painting. Of course it is a question of being able to recognise that sort of

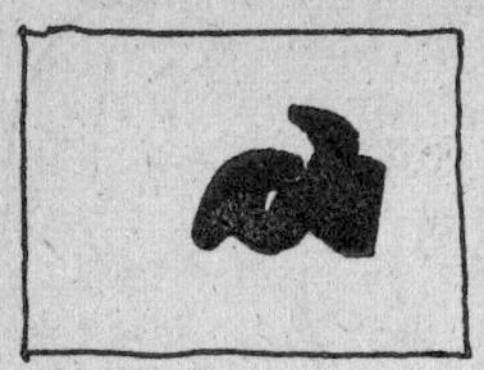

Fig. 13 Abstract painting – making a start.

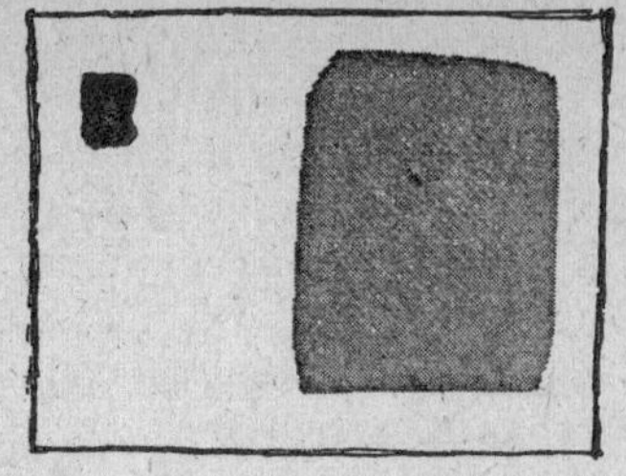

Fig. 14 Which do you think is the strongest area?

accident. As a scientist once said: 'Accident and chance favour only the trained mind.'

Or some part of the painting may have gone drastically wrong. This is when a palette knife is useful. To scrape and lift off any area of paint that is spoiling the rest.

With your effort, take a good look and add any colour that you think will improve the painting. The addition of more colour may mean you now have to change the earlier parts of the painting. A painting is a living thing, and always should be growing and changing.

Perhaps the result of abstract experiments may have got into a muddle. At any rate consciously and unconsciously you will have learnt a considerable amount about the feel and nature of oil paint. As much as learning about colour and tone and form, one should know the feel of paint. Every painter's response to the quality of paint itself is very different. Some painters like thin transparent paint. Others like to build up layers and become involved with the thick oily aspect of paint. After experiment, it may be that you get really excited by abstraction, and feel it has endless possibilities for self expression. So much the better, there is another chapter later dealing with further problems in abstraction. But it is still worth trying figurative paintings, as there are times when the problems are similar. Equally, abstract painting may not be right for you at the moment. You will, however, have discovered it is not as easy as one is tempted to think before one has tried. It is likely that the

movement in line
Rhythm leads
to movement.
This is based on
"The Dance" by
Matisse – 1910

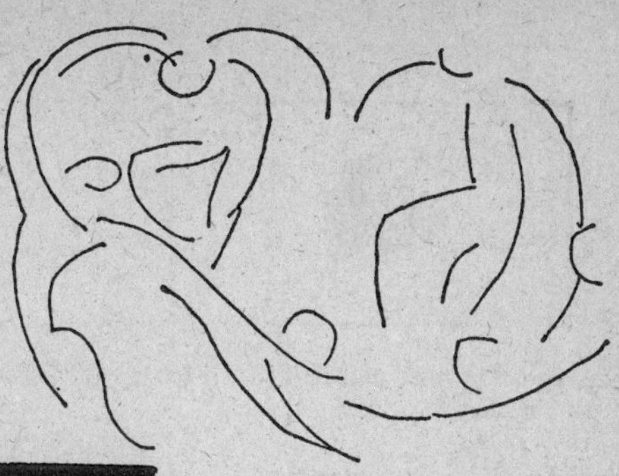

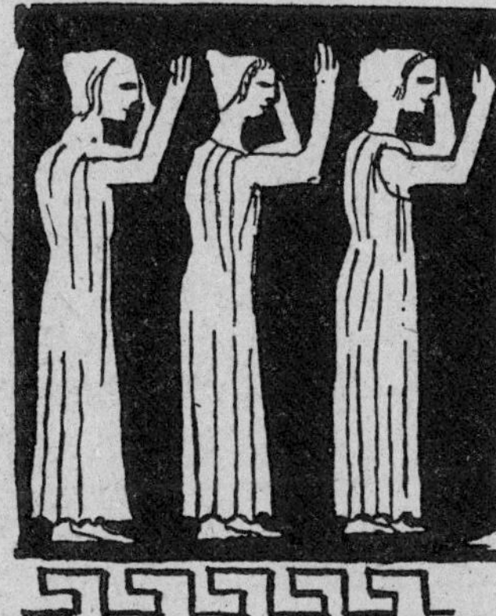

Rhythm based on repeat
pattern. From an archaic
vase

Rhythm based
on tones,

Guido Renis'
Aurora 1614

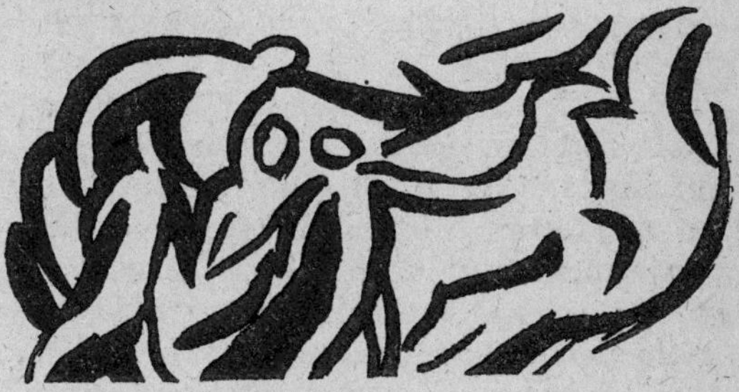

Fig. 15 Rhythm.

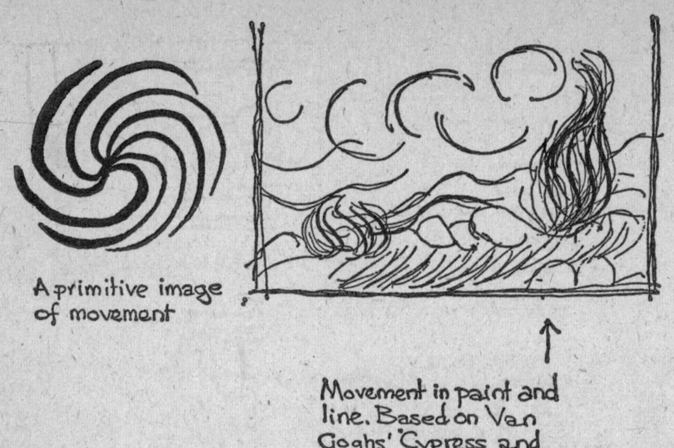

Fig. 16 Movement.

tendency to abstraction is inherent in some painters as it may be in whole peoples and cultures. In this way, abstract art can express fundamental causes that are inherent in most art forms.

YOU CAN EXPERIMENT WITH THESE

RHYTHM. A most basic cause. We walk in rhythm, our heart beat is life rhythm. Rhythm is the first cause of pattern (Fig. 15).

OTHER FORMS OF MOVEMENT. Swift brush strokes across your board to express speed and other forms of movement (Fig. 16).

THE STATIC AND ETERNAL. Shapes to express the static. Pure horizontals and vertical. These are the basic construction forms of man. The vertical and the horizontal are the beginnings of building (Fig. 17).

COLOUR TO EXPRESS MOOD. This was suggested in the last chapter on colour. It is worth experimenting. To some, blue with its association with sky, expresses peace. As red expresses fire. Or in some cultures, splendour.

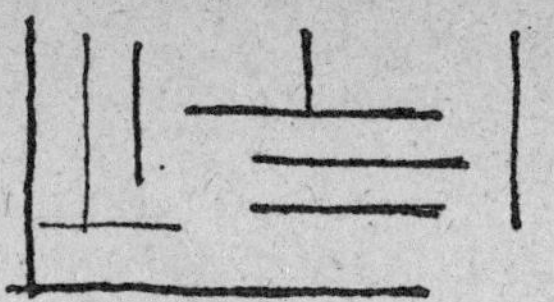

static forms are based on horizontals and verticals

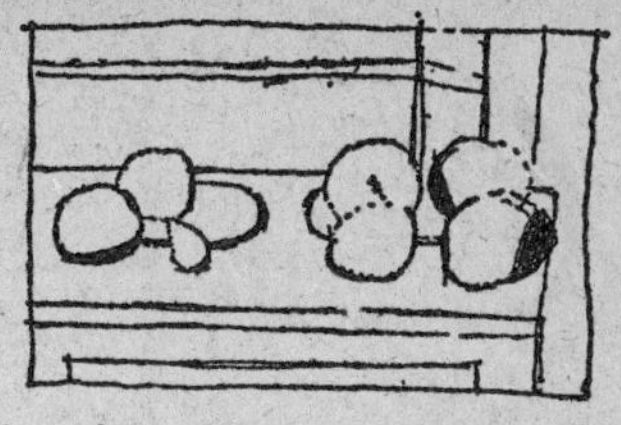

from a Still life by Cezanne

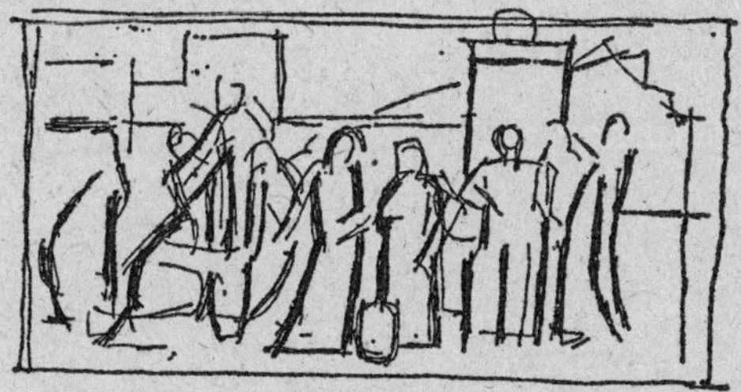

From Poussin's "Rebecca & Eliezer at the Well"

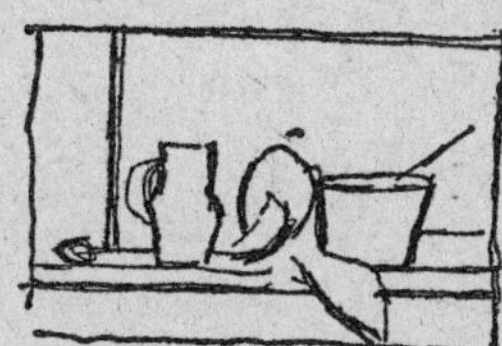

From a still life by Chardin in the Glasgow Art Gallery

Fig. 17 Static forms.

The first paintings you do may finally look nothing like what you originally had in mind. As one gets to know one's paints, the gap between what is in one's mind and what is possible in a painting narrows, until one is thinking in terms of paint.

A list of painters to look at in galleries or in picture books (either if you can):

Paul Klee, Swiss, 1879–1940.

Piet Mondrian, Dutch, 1872–1944.
Vassily Kandinsky, Russian, 1866–1944.
Ben Nicholson, British, 1894–.

SUGGESTED BOOKS FOR FURTHER READING

Kandinsky, The Thinking Eye by Paul Overy. Elek.

This book contains excellent text, reproductions and valuable quotations from Kandinsky's book that was a founding source of abstraction *Concerning the Spiritual in Art*, and his other writings.

Pedagogical Sketchbook by Paul Klee. Faber and Faber.

Paul Klee's classic book, the results of his teaching at the Bauhause. Painters still find it inspiring and moving.

TAILPIECE

Remember – after a day's painting, clean up!

CHAPTER SIX

STILL LIFE AND FLOWERS

Most painting handbooks advise a still life for one's first attempts at painting. This is really rather a good idea, as, providing the objects of the still life are durable, you can work on indefinitely. Also, many painters can express themselves and work much better, when they see their subject in front of them.

Still life painting emerged as an art form in its own right in seventeenth century Holland and Flanders. Its immediate ancestors were paintings of objects all chosen to remind the spectator of the fleeting vanity of mortal life. Previous to that, still life had only been incidental objects in figure composition. A great number of still lifes were painted in seven teenth century Holland. Very often an entirely unknown artist survives through one really great but small still life painting. It was usual in Holland at that time for painters to specialise in one particular kind of painting. This emerged as there was no demand in a Protestant country for religious painting. Dutch painters' attitudes to still life can inspire us today. They recorded beloved everyday objects, and possessions of a proud patron. Looking at them today we can admire the incredible skill of painters who could so accurately recreate texture by painting the fall of light on surfaces. To many people Dutch still lifes of flowers are the best known; unfortunately all too often in very bad imitations. This should not put us off the really good flower paintings which are miracles of care and accuracy. Light on surfaces is a constant that goes all the way through Dutch and Flemish painting, and oil paint is peculiarly suitable for this.

Chardin in France in the eighteenth century invested still life with a new quality of the eternity and monumentality.

Even so, the official art teaching and art theorists of Chardin's day, put still life as a lower form of art to the grand full-scale figure composition. This idea prevailed until Cézanne, who died in 1906. Cézanne raised still life to the level of figure composition. He used formally arranged still lifes to work out his theories of form, colour, and composition. Cézanne's still lifes repay any amount of study and copying. In the present century, the general trend of still life has been to make paintings patterns from simple objects of which we have a pre-knowledge, like bottles and fruit.

So much then for a brief history of the still life, now to start painting. First, before anything else, have your equipment ready. But what to paint? Many of the old fashioned painting manuals had, as a first exercise, a still life of a few simple forms in a limited colour range. This is a very good exercise, especially if the whole array of colours on your palette is a bit formidable at first sight. A fair selection of objects to begin with could include a couple of cylindrical earthenware crocks, a white ball or an egg, and one or two square or oblong carbboard boxes.

Here then are the objects of your painting. Now comes one of the basic problems of painting. Somehow or other these shapes of objects will have to fit into the area of your board. This is where composition comes in.

Set the pots, etc., on a table, mantelshelf, etc. where they will not be disturbed. If possible, see that it is a place where the light does not change. Lighting is worth taking care over, as an ever-changing light is very distracting. In the Western tradition of art the fall of light on a surface is the way we recognise solid form.

Obviously consistency is essential to our reading of a flat area conveying the idea of solid form (this is equally, and more so of a photograph).

So to work out a composition. This is where you will find a few drawings useful. It is possible to start painting without drawings to start, but it will save you a lot of trouble if you work things out first. Before following up in Chapter 7 about drawing for painting, consider the following.

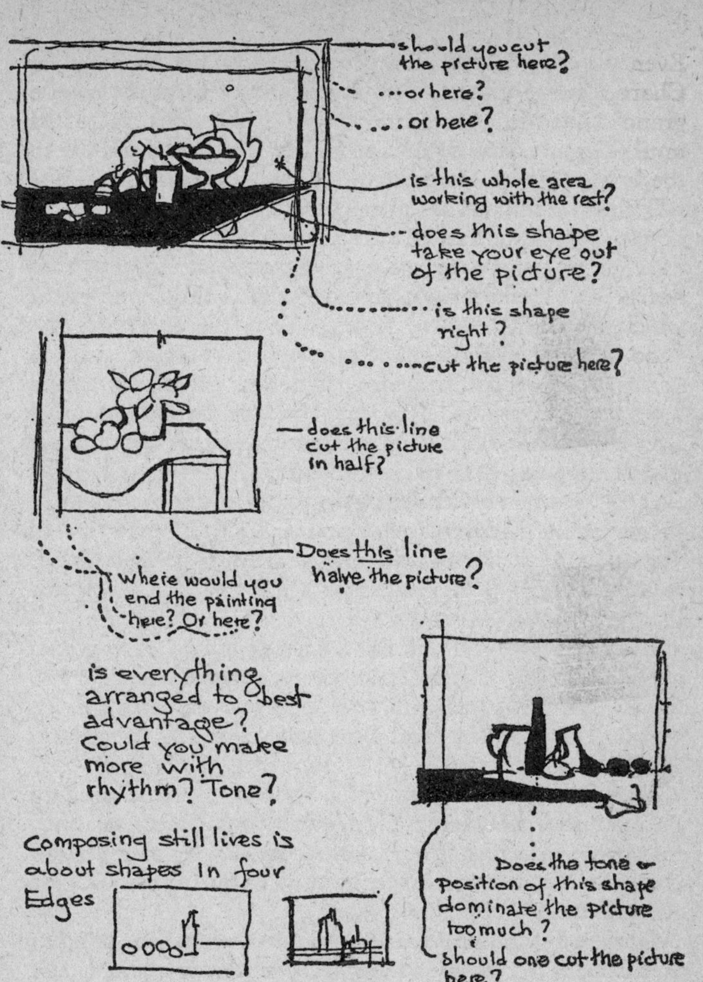

Fig. 18 The problems of composition.

Now to paint. With thin paint draw in the main areas. With equally thin paint – that is, your colours well diluted with turpentine and oil – cover in all the areas with the approximate colours. Get all the area of your board covered with paint as soon as possible, the white area of a board if you leave them unpainted are very distracting.

Always useful in any painting – and still life is no exception – is to paint the lightest areas and the darkest. This established, it gives you the key to the tonal range of the whole painting. Indeed, some painters make certain that any still life they paint contains an area of white by which to gauge all the other colours. In this painting, the colour range is deliberately restricted. Though, if you look carefully, greys and soft browns contain endless variety. To create the illusion of solidity with shadow, look at Fig. 19.

This kind of still life depicting objects that do not fade or go off (as fruit and flowers obviously do) has the advantage that it can be worked on until you really get it right. Give it a break and come back to it.

FORMALLY ARRANGED STILL LIFES

If problems of formal composition appeal to you, a very good way of studying this is to arrange very complex still lifes. Fig. 20 gives some suggestions based on classic compositions.

Even if the idea of formally composing a still life is not the way you feel about still life, however informally or otherwise still life is approached, you cannot escape the problem of arranging shapes within the four sides of your board. This is the basis of composition.

Perhaps the most usual and excellent reason for painting a still life is in order to take delight in the variety of objects around us – fine old pots, fruit, vases, glass, and so forth. Here, therefore, is a few words about painting them:

When painting china and glass, the highlights are the lightest things you see. Their equivalent on your board will be the white paint, which will not be anything like as bright as the actual light itself, of course. This means that all the

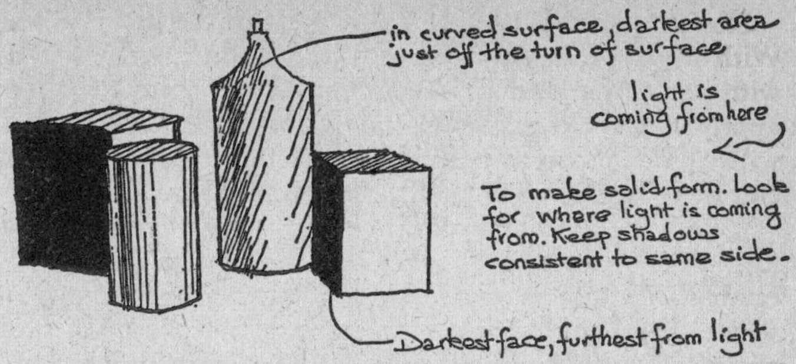

Fig. 19 Creating the illusion of solidity.

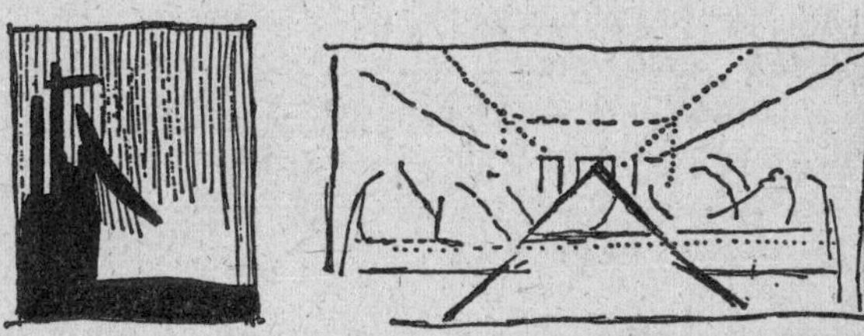

light, dark, or middle tones from Rembrandt's Lament.

The triangular composition. Lines of perspective to take your eye right into the painting. from Leonardo's Last Supper

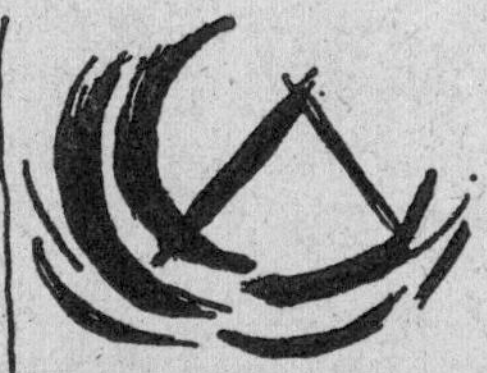

Concentric and triangular. based on a sketch by Poussin

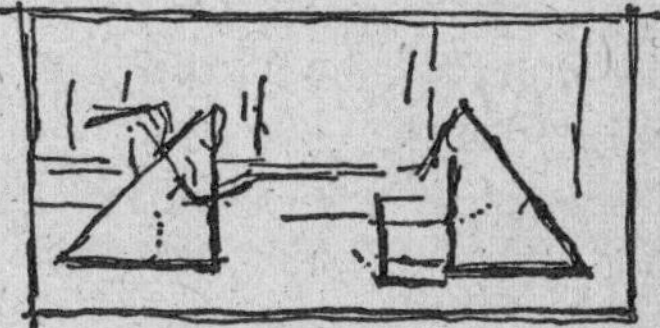

Equal Balanced composition from Leonardo's Annunciation

Fig. 20 Formal composition.

other tones in the painting have to be scaled accordingly. It is tempting in a painting to save highlights to the last, as finishing touches. In fact this never works, as the highlights jump out, and put the rest of the painting out of key.

The sensual quality of fruit rightly appeals to painters – a painter like Cézanne could make a whole universe out of a few apples. The secret of clear bright colour is quite simple. It consists in keeping your colour clean. As soon as colour gets dirty on the palette, scrape it off and put out a fresh lot.

As in any sort of painting, you should begin with colours well thinned in turpentine and oil, and build up thicker. Build up all areas of the painting evenly. It is easy in a still life to get so carried away by one object that the rest of the board gets forgotten. Stand right away from your painting every so often while you are working – a part that looks somewhat empty may easily look better when you have added more paint. If in doubt what to paint on any part of your painting do not go on mixing indefinitely on the palette. Be brave and put some paint on; it will look better than none at all.

In still lifes, or anything else, shadows are darker, but at all times look for colour on shadows. Often they are the complementary colour mentioned in Chapter 7 but if you do not actually see them, you should paint what you *do* see. The true colour of the object in front of you should be painted by the simplest method; it is never a good idea to mix colour for the sake of so doing, as this is the first way that colours become dense and muddy. Take care too about dipping into white paint. This should not be automatic, as white paint in shadows is one of the first things that can make a painting look muddy and heavy. Sometimes, when one stands back and considers one's painting the result is dreadfully disappointing. Paradoxically, this is the time to take heart. Never be timid about drastically re-altering and repainting whole parts of paintings. A painting is a living, growing thing, and change never does any harm. If there is something that is not quite right in a painting and you cannot make up your mind where the fault lies, it is useful to turn the painting upside down. Or, if you really feel all is in a hopeless mess and the surface is refusing even to be worked on (and this can happen), put the painting away and come to it fresh after a week or so.

It is quite possible too, that one can get very brilliant beginnings to paintings, the result of an entirely spontaneous response to the subject. You could leave it as it is, but this might lead to the dangerous habit of never finishing anything. It is probably better to be brave and go on. At all times criticise your own work. Ask the following questions:

Are the tones of each colour working to make a harmonious whole?

Is each shape working well with the other shapes?

Are there areas of the painting where the density of the paint is too light or too heavy for the rest?

Is one part painted in such intense detail that it 'puts out' all the other painting and has to be taken away with palette knife. This in fact often happens – the very portion of the painting that had most carried one away, is the portion that distorts the rest!

SOME MORE SUGGESTIONS FOR USING PAINT IN STILL LIFE

Glazing is delightful in painting the colours of fruit, or indeed anything else. For example, a patch of yellow can be left to dry. Then it can be painted over lightly with an entirely transparent layer of green or red, to give a luminous effect. In reverse, dark colours allowed to dry a bit, and then glazed over with white, give unusual and subtle greys. Try painting a still life with palette knife. A palette knife not only puts paint on in slabs of varying thickness, it also can be used on the board to work in the paint. Palette knives or painting knives also make a smooth and polished surface which can be used for glazing on, to great effect.

STILL LIFES THAT ARE NOT ARRANGED

It is not essential to arrange a still life formally. Once your eye is trained to look out for these things, one can see

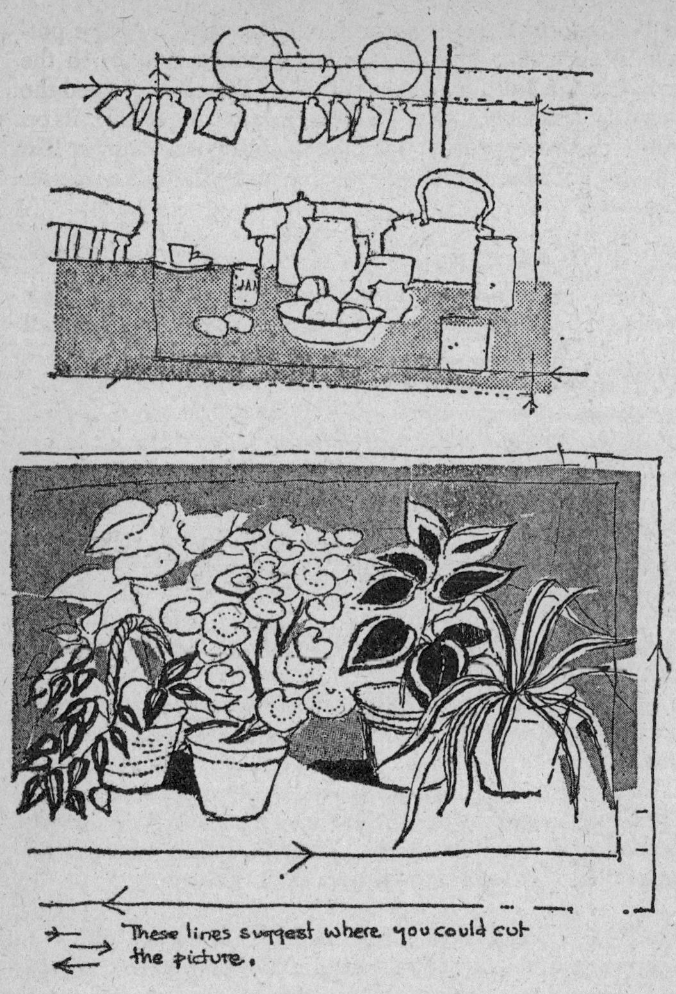

Fig. 21 Random subjects for still life painting.

still lifes form themselves, as it were by chance. Some pot-plants on a sill, china on a mantelpiece, are as much the making of a still life as anything else. Bonnard painted the most splendid still lifes of the chance gathering of utensils on tables. However, once you come to transpose a subject like this to your board, your very choice immediately eliminates accident.

FLOWER PAINTING

Flower painting is a branch of still life painting, but there are one or two differences that give flower painting rules all its own. One of them is that it is quite possible to paint very good flower paintings even if one is hopeless at painting everything else one attempts. Another is, that one usually gets the problem of a highly concentrated area against a comparatively less complex background. One also finds this in portraits, and it brings problems that cannot be disregarded.

Finally of course, flowers impose a time limit. The very impermanence of flowers often inspires bright and spontaneous paintings, just painting away in the way that children do, without much serious thought about accuracy of drawing or anything else. Sometimes these sort of paintings are not really much like flowers and are only splashes of paint. Perhaps there is no harm in this, if you enjoy doing it, and the results give somebody else pleasure. However, there is the unmistakable danger that unless you impose some sort of discipline on your work, these sort of paintings do not get better, and only get worse. The discipline one should employ is to make careful drawings of flowers.

FLOWER PAINTING IN THE DUTCH MANNER

Some painters rightly wish to paint flowers very accurately as the old Dutch painters did. In this case you should use a board with at least two or three coats of priming, and use sable, kolinsky or ox-hair brushes to get a really smooth effect. On no account be tempted to make flowers up, as this proves most unsatisfactory. Design of the plants and

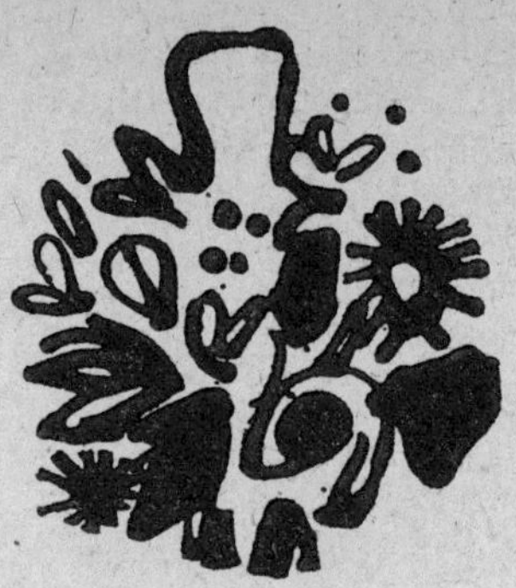

Fig. 22 A splashy flower painting can be fun – but it can also get a bit much!

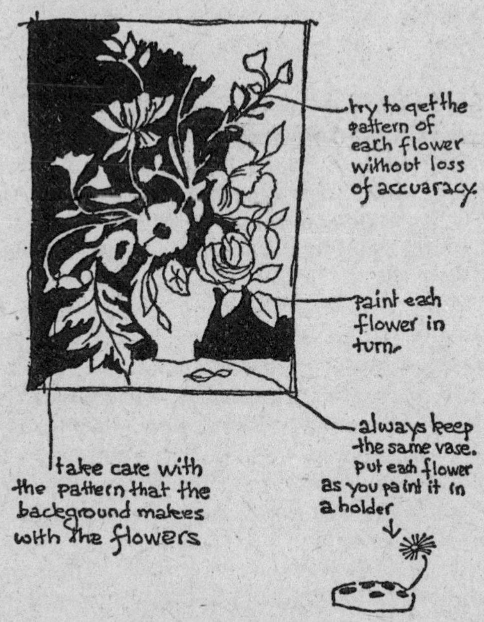

Fig. 23 Painting flowers.

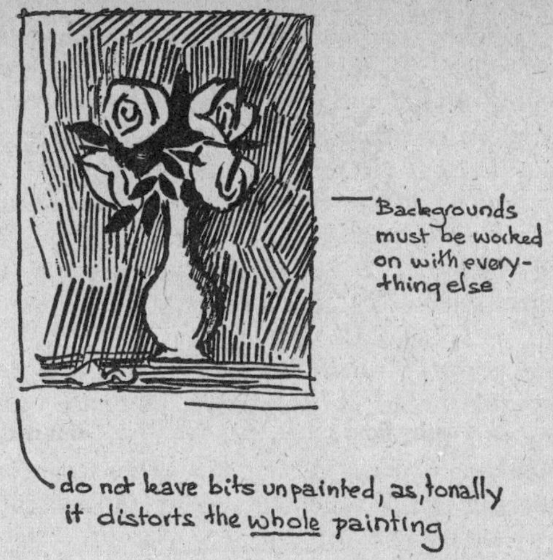

Fig. 24 Backgrounds.

flowers against the background should be well thought-out, making sure that there is a lively and interesting pattern of shapes of flowers against the background. Each flower is painted in turn, sparing no trouble to get every detail accurate. There are some painters who, in their nature, respond to detail and intricacy, and enjoy reproducing light on surfaces.

The technique described for meticulous flower painting could equally well be used for other still life subjects. One could paint flowers in the Dutch manner on a dark ground. But even if you use a dark ground, underneath that there should be a light base to prevent colours darkening in time. So far two very different and opposite approaches to flower painting have been described. Generally, however, most people's paintings fall somewhere between the entirely spontaneous and the highly meticulous.

FLOWER PAINTING GENERALLY

The glazing technique described earlier in this chapter is also particularly suitable for flowers. The quinacridone colours glazed over whites and creams are delightful for painting roses. Painting-wise, and nothing to do with botany, flowers fall into more or less two types: the clear and contained forms of flowers like tulips, paeonies and roses, and then the more diffused forms one finds in daisies and bunches of wild flowers. Be careful when painting the latter not to get the painting too spotty. Try handling your paint so that its surface appears as though it is detailed, although the effect is only the way you have put the paint on the board.

When painting flowers, whatever the composition, the background should be painted at the same time as the flowers, and not left as an afterthought. The result will never look right if you do not remember this. No one part of a painting can be touched without it immediately affecting every other part.

SOME SUGGESTIONS FOR UNUSUAL COLOURS BY MIXING AND GLAZING

Greys can be mixed by cobalt and light red and white.

Greys can be mixed by purple and raw umber and white.

Greys can be mixed by cerulean and cadmium red and white.

Greys can be mixed by viridian and either rose or crimson and white.

Luminous red by glazing cadmium red on an orange ground.

Luminous purple by glazing purple over a pink.

Luminous jade green by glazing viridian and a touch of white over lemon yellow.

Out of all these possibilities of approaching still life it is to be hoped that you will find your own personal interpretation. If, for some reason, your experiments in still life have been disappointing, on no account worry. It is certain that you will reap the results in something else. Until you have tried a subject you cannot really know whether you will take to it, but the work is never in vain. Of course, the reverse may be the case – you may have distilled on the flat surface of your board, some permanent record of a favourite object.

At the beginning, do not worry about doing good paintings, they will come in time. Painting should be done for its own sake, whatever the outcome. The outcome at any time may be quite unexpected.

BOOKS FOR FURTHER READING

Starting to Paint Still Life by Bernard Dunstan, R.A. Studio Vista.

Flower Painting For Beginners by Kenneth Jameson. Studio Vista.

TAILPIECE

Very good still lifes and flower paintings have often been done by little known or anonymous artists. This is one of the reasons why they are inspiring. These sort of paintings can be found in surprising places and small museums. Look out for them. Here is a list of still lifes and flower paintings by the greatest masters:

Cambridge, Fitzwilliam Museum: P. Bonnard, *Still Life;* P. Claez, *Still Life.*

Edinburgh, National Gallery: Chardin, *Vase of Flowers;* Kalf, *Still Life;* Fantin-Latour, *Roses.*

Glasgow Art Gallery: Cézanne, *Overturned Basket of Fruit.*

Newcastle Laing Art Gallery: Ruskin Spear, *Still Life With Fishes.*

York City Art Gallery: Mendendez, *Still Life With Lemons and Nuts.*

London, Tate Gallery: Morandi, *Still Life;* Cézanne, *Still Life with Water Jug* (unfinished); William Nicholson, *Mushrooms.*

London, National Gallery: Vuillard, *Mantelshelf;* Gauguin, *Flowers;* Fantin-Latour, *Roses.*

The two British painters Duncan Grant and Matthew Smith are excellent painters of still life. They are well represented in most city art galleries. Anne Redpath should also be looked out for, though she is better represented in her native Scotland than in the south. The same is so of the Scottish painter Peploe. There are two Cézanne still lifes in the Courtauld Institute, London.

CHAPTER SEVEN

DRAWING FOR PAINTING

This chapter is about drawing for painting. That is: the kind of drawings that are intended specifically as working drawings for paintings. This may sound a bit obvious, but there are other kinds of drawing that are executed just for their own sake. Some beginners take endless trouble to perfect a technique of drawing that is quite separate from their painting. We are all familiar with a kind of drawing that has elegant lines and slick cross hatching, which many people believe is 'good drawing'. It may indeed be so, but such drawings are useless enough when one actually comes to paint from them.

In painting, one is very dependent upon drawings – to record things one will never see again and wants to turn into a painting, to work out a composition, for details, and many other reasons. The point about working out compositions is worth repeating, as it reminds one of the French word for drawing, *dessin*. This of course implies the element of design that should be inherent in any drawing. It also makes the saying, usually so off-putting, that one 'must be able to draw before one can paint', make a bit more sense. One hears this said often enough, and usually by people who do not paint. This is heretical by some standards, but painting and drawing are indistinguishable, and should not be considered apart; it is best to learn both together. Which is why I suggested that one should begin by painting and draw later.

EQUIPMENT

A half Imperial drawing board.

A pair of cardboard 'L' shapes (see Fig. 25).

These are adjusted to make a sort of view finder, and are very useful.

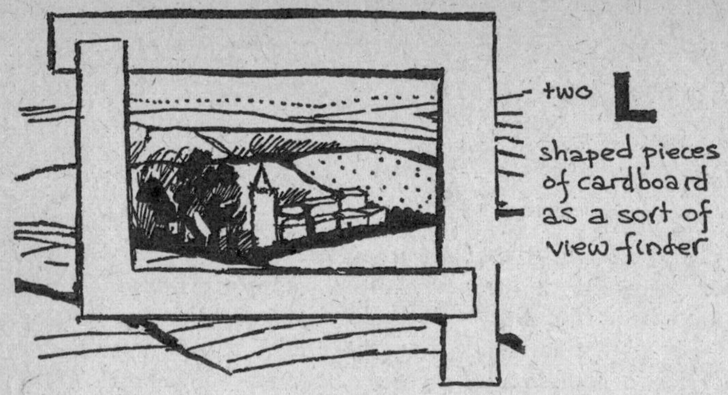

Fig. 25 Cardboard 'L' shapes.

Any sort of paper you like, though it is not really necessary to buy expensive water colour paper. Student cartridge is perfectly good. A small pocket sketch book to take down the unexpected thing, or whatever fleetingly takes your fancy.

Pencils. The most convenient for taking around. As you know, they come in a range of hardness and softness. Hard pencils are useful for detailed drawings, like flowers or buildings. Soft pencils are better for working quickly. However, you must use whatever you find suits you the best.

Charcoal and Conté chalk are the traditional drawing materials. They are soft, and make a delightful mark on paper. They are inclined to smudge which can be used as an advantage, but would obviously be inconvenient if you were drawing out-of-doors, unless you were very careful. You can get greater tonal range with charcoal and conté than with any grade of paper pencil. Charcoal and conté can be sharpened to a very fine point. To prevent either from smudging too badly, they may be sprayed with fixative. This has, however, the disadvantage of spoiling the surface by making it go flat and dead.

Pen and Ink has great tonal range. The best nibs are the old fashioned long ones you can find in banks. Buy them

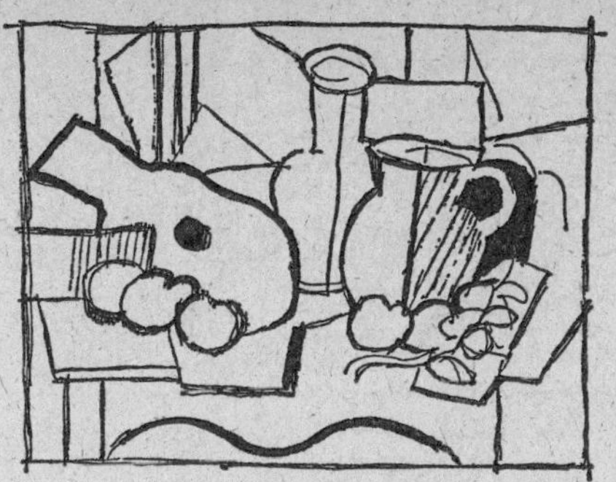

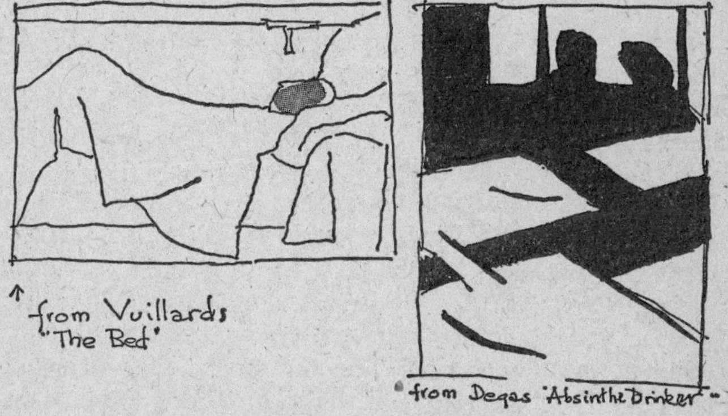

Fig. 26 Remember – drawing is about shapes in the picture space in relation to the edges. These are examples from modern painters. Make your own experiments with the same idea.

when you can, as they are gradually disappearing from general use. They have the great advantage of range of line, from the thin and incisive to the broad line if you press hard. Very good pens can be made by cutting reeds or garden canes. These make very vigorous lines on the paper. Examples of their use can be seen in Japanese drawings and the later drawings of Van Gogh.

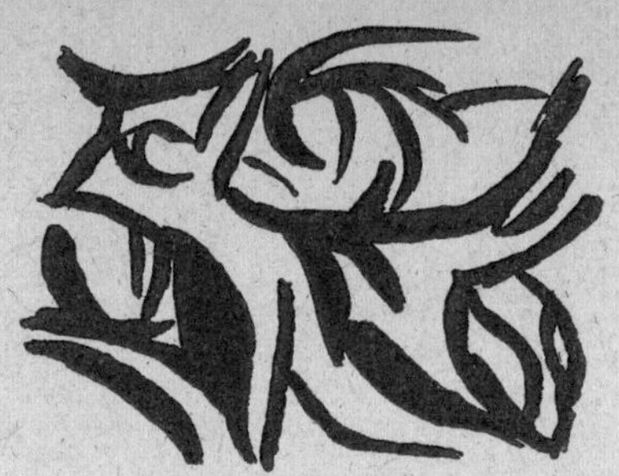

Fig. 27 Lines of rhythm.

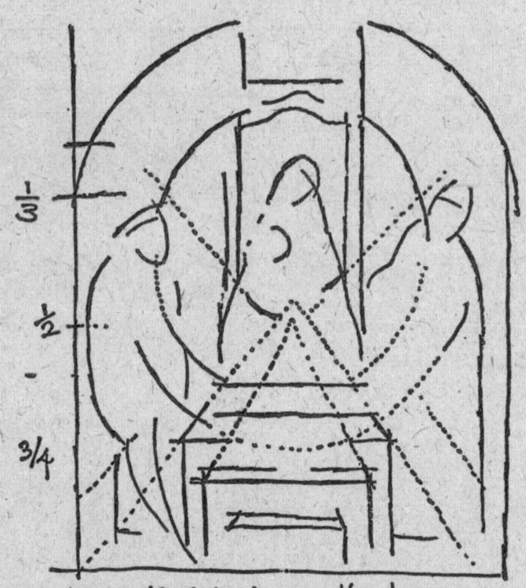

Lines that make up the basic composition and geometry of Raphaels' "Ansidei Madonna." One of the great classic compositions.

Fig. 28 Lines that make up basic shapes: taken from Raphael's 'Ansidei Madonna'. This composition is inexhaustible for copying and study.

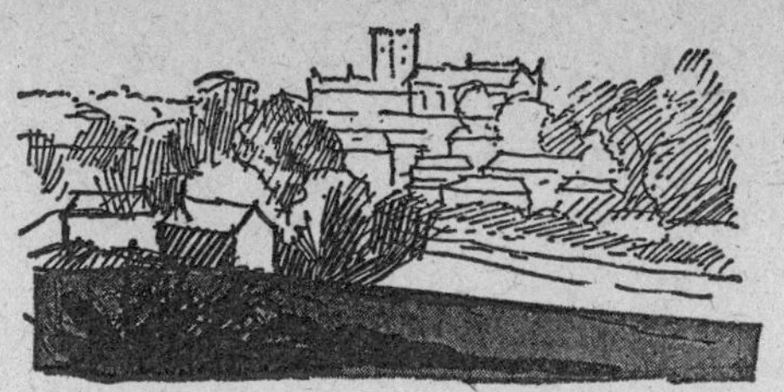

Fig. 29 The nearer to you, the sharper the tonal contrasts!

Brush and Ink. This is a technique of drawing for painting that can be highly recommended to a beginner. Using a brush to draw accustoms one to think of one's drawings in terms of painting from the beginning.

In the end you have to find your own method and techniques. W. R. Sickert, who made the most intricate and excellent drawings for paintings, used several media on one drawing.

From the start, do not be worried or put off by the thought that you may not be able to draw. Very often artists who develop a facility for drawing become so carried away by their skill that they stop looking closely. Also, it is better to make a rather halting and clumsy drawing that is all your own than a clever imitation of somebody else's.

To start then:

First think about shapes.

All the parts of the painting in relation to the edges of the painting (Fig. 26).

Think about lines of rhythm in the composition (Fig. 27).

Lines to make up basic shape of composition (Fig. 28).

Drawing for a painting helps you work out your doubts and mistakes, so that they are eliminated from the painting.

TONES

Earlier, we established that tones in a painting are what would come out in shades of grey if the painting were photographed. Tonality is of great importance in drawings that are to be used for paintings.

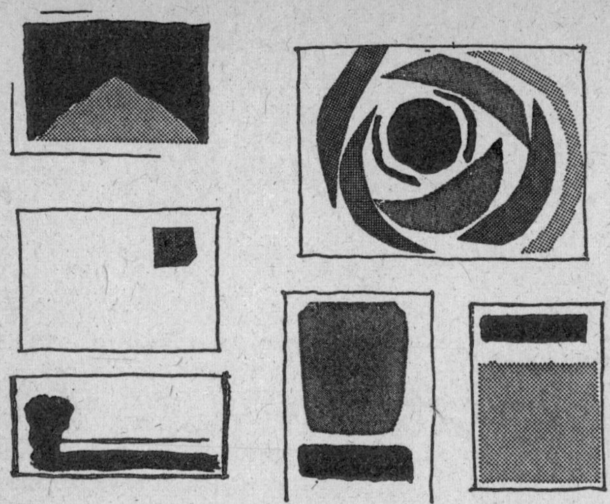

Fig. 30 Tonal balance is essential.

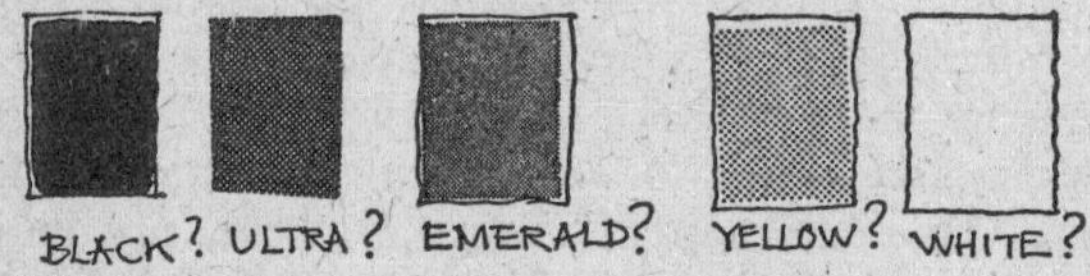

Fig. 31 Some attempt to give tonal equivalents between black and white. Try this for yourself.

Tones affect the whole balance of a composition, as well as giving solid form.

In a landscape they give distance (Fig. 29). Even in a painting that is quite without tonality to express distance or solid form, the tonal balance of each colour's tones is essential (Fig. 30). Chapter 4 gives tonal depths of each colour. When you are making a tonal drawing for a painting try to approximate the tonal value of every colour (Fig. 31).

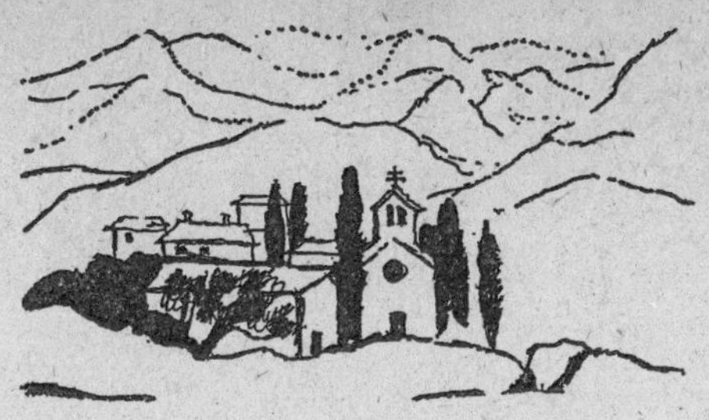

Fig. 32 The buildings give scale to the landscape. The works of man are the measure of landscape.

DRAWING FOR LANDSCAPE

Unless one works very fast, or one is consistently lucky with the weather, a considerable amount of landscape painting is done in studios away from the subject, and therefore most likely from drawings.

Lines of composition and tonality have been dealt with; they give one the broad masses of the whole. What one will almost certainly need as well, are careful drawings of certain details to give the painting authenticity. These sort of details might be accurate drawings of trees, foreground vegetation and rocks. Also, if the landscape includes buildings, you will want drawings of these, not only in architectural detail, but notes of the buildings in relation to the general scale of the landscape (Fig. 32).

DRAWING FOR PORTRAITS

Before starting a portrait a few drawings are a very good idea to get to know the face of your subject. Draw the face as in Fig. 33.

Then decide which view is most like your subject. The classic rules for measuring heads, which have been used by portrait painters since about the Italian Renaissance, are as useful now as they were then (Fig. 34). But the head is only a part of the whole painting.

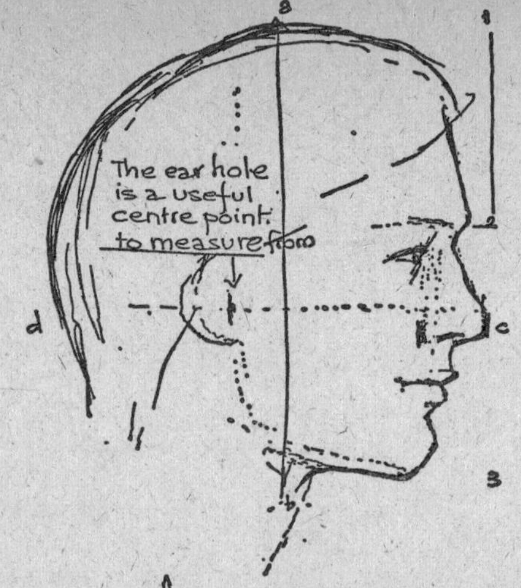

measure heads greatest length - line a/b
to heads' greatest breadth line c/d
length of brow line 1/2
in proportion to line 2/c
line 2/c in relation to line c/3
measure where is mouth line between C and 3
A profile tells you about a full face

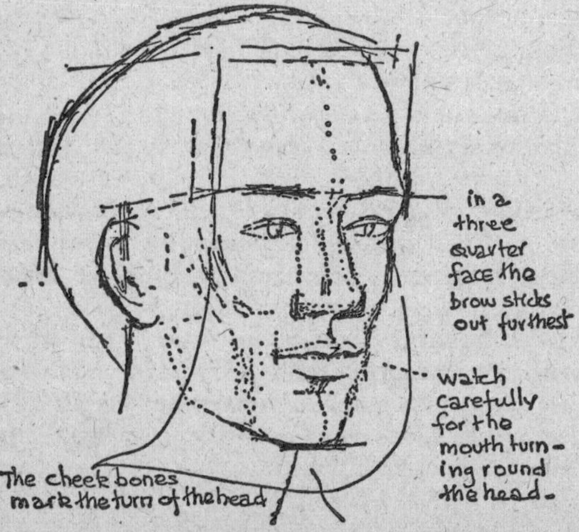

Fig. 33 Drawing a face.

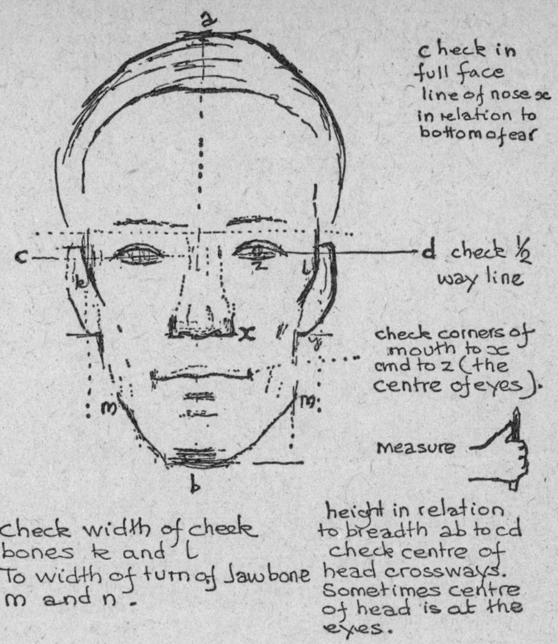

Fig. 34 Measurements for the head.

COMPOSING A PORTRAIT

Even if you try to avoid it, the head will always dominate a portrait. Indeed, with this limitation you have to compose the picture accordingly. The shapes that are left out have to be managed with ingenuity and care.

Detailed drawings of hands, clothing etc. are essential if you have a limited number of sittings. Never worry if drawings for paintings look rather a mess. The whole idea of a drawing is that you are working out your ideas and exploring the subject generally. Drawings for paintings are intensely personal, and so long as they are helpful to you, not much else matters. This means that the more you paint

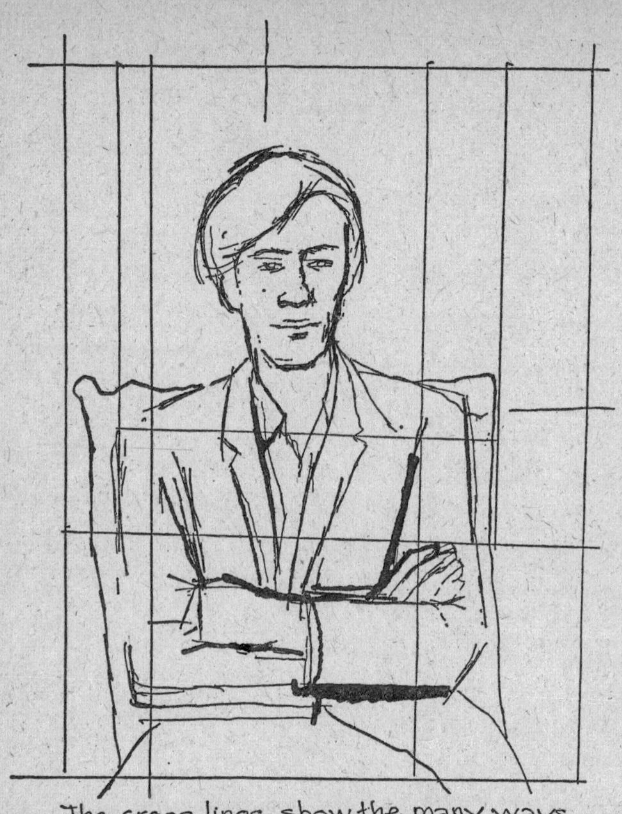

Fig. 35 The cross lines show the many ways you can compose a portrait
What you leave outside the head is as important as the head.

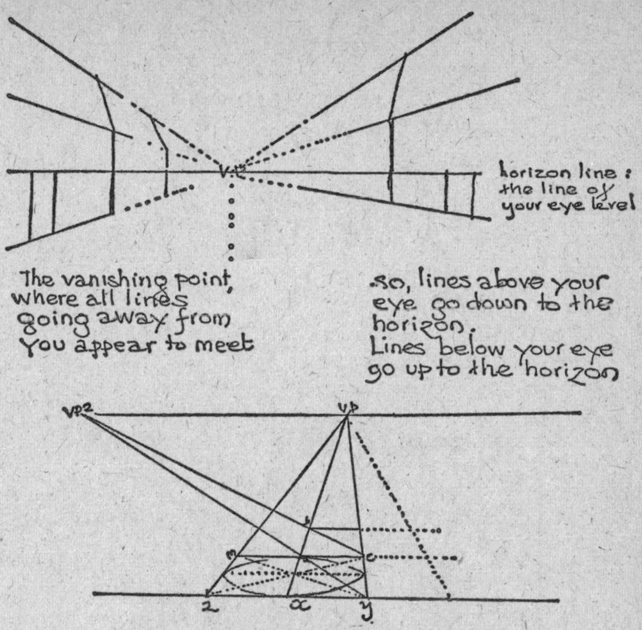

To draw tiles, pillars etc. going away from you

Join VP at x and at y
Join y to a and produce to Vp2
at a draw line parallell to xy to meet line vpy at c
Join VP2 to c, to cross line xVP at b
at b, draw line parallel to ac to meet line vpy at d
and so on

To make a circle in perspective
let zx = xy, join VP to z
continue line ca to meet line VP2 at m
Join cz, and join my. Where they cross, draw a line parallel to zy. Draw a circle and so on.

Fig. 36 Perspective.

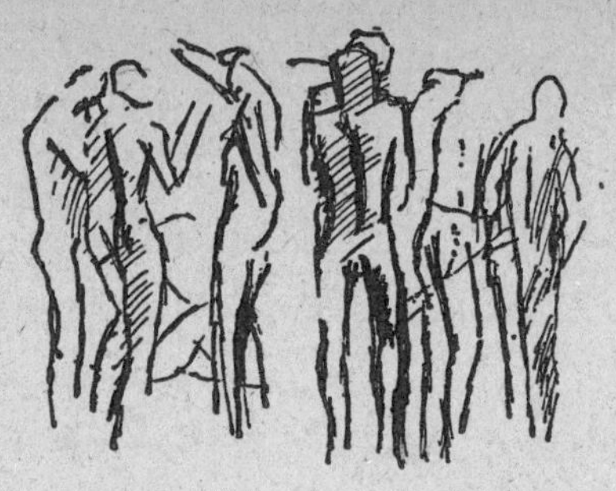

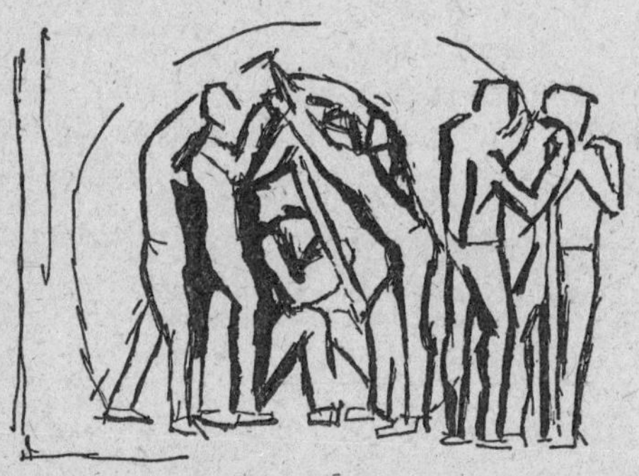

Fig. 37 This is just a suggestion – perhaps you would have approached it some other way!

and draw, the more you will develop a technique of drawing that is in terms of your painting.

The one department of drawing where there are fixed rules is perspective. Many painters nowadays do without perspective altogether, but if architectural studies are in your vision of things, then it is an essential. I freely admit that the more complicated branches of perspective are quite beyond me and I have always made do with the basic rules shown in Fig. 36. However, the book list at the end of the chapter gives you more advanced works on the subject if you feel like studying it further.

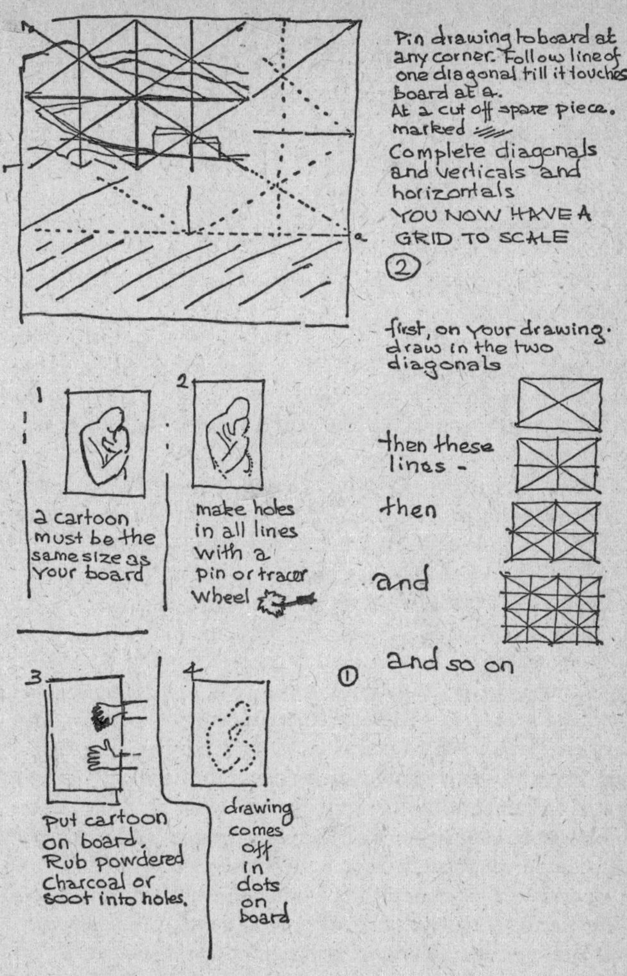

Fig. 38 Transferring a drawing in accurate scale.

DRAWINGS FOR FORMAL FIGURE COMPOSITIONS

The formal compositions of the old masters do not appear to be practised much by painters today, though this is no reason whatever for not doing so if you want to. The formal figure compositions were usually painted entirely from a series of drawings, starting from sketches from life, and gradually worked into a painting (Fig. 37).

The method for transferring a drawing in accurate scale to your board is shown in Fig. 38. Or, if your drawing were the correct size, it could be done by the cartoon method (also see Fig. 38).

Naturally, you do not have to begin every painting with a drawing, and it is sometimes a good thing to not do so at all, but you will find your own way as you go one. Drawing is painting without the colour and it trains the eye. The chapter on flowers recommended the devoted painter of flowers to do drawings every so often to train the eye entirely for botanical studies. In this case, you should use a hard, sharp pencil, and treat the drawing as a systematic study of the anatomy of the plant (Fig. 39).

Remember it is always a good idea to carry a sketch book. Continual drawing trains the eye to see. A very good exercise in learning to see is to try, in front of a subject, to banish all words from one's mind, and to see the subject in terms of tone and line etc. We are so accustomed from our earliest childhood to naming objects we see that this can impose, even unconsciously, barriers to seeing.

Here is a list of painters whose drawings well repay study. They are chosen because their drawing methods are so much in terms of their paintings.

Rembrandt. Dutch School 1606–69. Rembrandt made thousands of drawings which should be looked at with his paintings, to see how closely they inter-relate.

Peter Paul Rubens. 1577–1640. Flemish School. Rubens was one of the most brilliant draughtsmen who ever lived, and his methods of painting are in the same terms as his drawings.

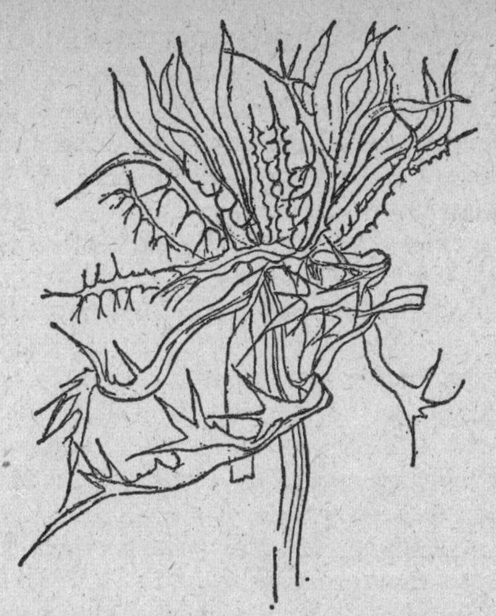

Fig. 39 Drawing for botanical study.

Nicolas Poussin. 1593–1665. French Roman. Through Poussin's drawings the complete process of making a painting can be traced. It is as though one were watching the artist work.

John Constable. 1776–1837. British School. There was no aspect of nature that Constable did not explore in numerous sketches and drawings. He used a wide variety of methods and materials.

Vincent Van Gogh. 1853–90. Dutch School. Van Gogh's drawings with reed pens are strikingly similar to the way he uses a paintbrush.

The same can be said of the pencil drawings of *Paul Cézanne*. 1839–1906, French School.

Walter Richard Sickert. 1860–1942. British School. Many of Sickert's paintings were painted entirely from drawings. As an exercise, it is a good idea to do some drawings with the view to producing a painting from them, using nothing else.

THE FOLLOWING BOOKS WILL BE USEFUL

Basic Design, The Dynamics of Visual Form by Maurice de Sausmarez. Studio Vista.

Perspective by Hugh Chevins. Studio Vista. Also in the same series are excellent handbooks on drawing a whole variety of subjects.

Grammar of Drawing for Artists and Designers by Colin Hayes. Studio Vista.

Pedagogical Sketchbook by Paul Klee. Faber and Faber.

TAILPIECE

A useful comment on drawing by Delacroix: 'Just the thing that makes of a sketch the essential expression of the idea, is not the suppression of details, but their complete subordination to the big lines.'

Paul Klee reminds me – and I should have put this in earlier – that drawing can be about line. The line can just be for its own sake, going where it will. A line need not draw something from the external world. A line can be just itself. So can a tone or any other mark made by pencil or paint.

CHAPTER EIGHT

LANDSCAPE

When one enumerates the very greatest landscape painters, one discovers they flourished between the beginning of the sixteenth century till about the first decade of the present century. A possible explanation was that man's knowledge of nature was contained within landscape. Man's vision of the universe had not extended to outerspace, or at the other extreme to the world of the atom or molecule. Most people in those three hundred years lived much more directly in contact with landscape and nature. In the latter half of the twentieth century can one do landscape painting, where the landscapes we see are mostly quite unlike the landscape familiar to Constable or even the Impressionists? A landscape painter today is presented with two possible kinds of approach; either to accept that man has drastically altered the face of nature, and create a new vision of man in nature. Or to find the constants that are in landscape at all times – or, of course, a combination of both these.

Many artists' first response to the external world was through landscape. Beginners to painting, perhaps, have had a happy association with a landscape and it has inspired them to want to paint. It is worth quoting one of the letters of Constable, to whom, in any discussion on landscape, it is impossible not to refer. He wrote, 'painting with me is another word for feeling, and my association with my carefree boyhood made me a painter and I am glad.' In Constable's day, poets and painters found in nature reflection of their moods, and there are many of us today who find the same kind of inspiration from landscape.

For a beginner to painting, landscape has the immediate advantage that one usually sees or remembers a stretch of landscape as a whole. You do not get the problems of backgrounds, as in still life and flowers. There are other problems of course, and while discussing them, I shall assume for the first part of the chapter that you will be working more or less directly from nature, and not painting abstracts from landscape. Later in the chapter I shall deal with abstraction from landscape.

Before all else, it is as well to be practical, and think about organising landscape painting. Work out how much time you will have on the subject. If you live in the country, this is not nearly such a problem as if you live in town and are either going out on expeditions or on holiday. Always take into account that seasons, apart from changing the colour of landscape, also change the light. This is of course more true in the northern hemisphere than the Mediterranean and the South. Unless you are prepared to carry a painting over from year to year, nature itself will impose limits on time. The delights and yet the difficulty of painting in a country like Britain is the ever-changing light and weather.

Before you begin, check that you have all your equipment. Nothing is more aggravating than going on a landscape painting expedition and finding that you have left a vital colour or something behind.

METHODS OF APPROACH

You could do several drawings, small oil sketches from your subject, and build them up into a large painting at home. This was the method employed by Constable. It is fashionable to prefer the preliminary sketches because our eyes are conditioned by the Impressionist painters, but to really understand Constable, the sketches should be thought of as they were intended. This will make them not only more comprehensible, but more helpful in learning about Constable's methods.

PAINTING ONLY FROM NATURE

The Impressionist painters, Monet, Renoir, Pissaro and Sisley, were so concerned with representation of the way we see light and colour that they would only paint from nature directly. This gives Impressionist paintings their beautiful freshness that still delights us to this day. If one only wants to paint directly from the subject, one has either to work very fast or on a small scale, unless one is prepared to take the risk that one will find the same effects another time. In the north one takes the risk that nothing will ever be quite the same, though if one is painting in the Mediterranean one can repeatedly return to the subject without worrying that the light will alter. Australian artists have told me that the same is true there.

OTHER APPROACHES

A great number of painters approach landscape painting somewhere between these two methods. They may begin from the subject and then finish in the studio. It is quite usual for painters to have a paradoxical approach to nature, that the diversity and colours after a certain point in working from nature become distracting. Bonnard, the last of the landscape painters in the European tradition, wrote on one occasion 'The presence of the object, the *motiv*, can be most embarrassing for the artist.' So, if after painting outside, it all becomes a bit much, it is quite reasonable to finish the painting away from the subject.

As suggested in the last chapter, drawings could be used to work out the composition of a landscape, the finished drawing being transferred to your board. Then you could go on from sketches, and/or nature.

When you make drawings for landscape paintings, you find that very soon you come across one of the most fundamental and yet most absorbing problems of painting from nature. That is the duality of truth in a painting. What may be entirely true to external nature, may look quite wrong in a painting. One continually struggles and finally resolves a compromise between what the surface of the board and canvas demand and yet what is true to fact. As far as we can see, three of the greatest landscape painters who ever lived painted in this way. These painters are Pieter Breughel, Claude and Constable.

LIGHT IN LANDSCAPE

Constable wrote in about 1822 that 'the sky is the source of light in nature and governs everything, even our common observations on the weather of every day are suggested by it.' This statement is an excellent starting point for thinking about light. It is true that the sky is the light source, but it is not necessarily the lightest thing in the landscape. The lightest part of landscape can be reflected sky on water, or buildings. If you are at all familiar with landscapes in hot countries, the sky is often darker than the land and the buildings, making a beautiful blue against which everything is staged. Snow can be the lightest part. In any climate, morning light and afternoon light change the colours and shadows of the landscape. If you are working for a whole day at a time, do one lot of work in the morning and another in the afternoon. A completely cloudy day evens out light and tonality.

While you are painting light is constantly changing a little. Once your painting is well on its way, settle for a constant light. You will learn how to do this from experience.

The white on your palette is the nearest equal you have to the lightest part of the landscape. To give the lightest parts their truest intensity in terms of the painting, it is often necessary to intensify the darks. Light to some painters, especially Turner was a primal element, he was obsessed by light, air and water. He was, however, equally obsessed by his paint, and the greatness of his paintings are because his eye and medium have achieved such a marvellous closeness. Here then are some ideas from Turner to paint skies:

A thick layer of white or pale yellow, laid on with palette knife, and glazed with transparent reds.

Swift, broad brush strokes to convey the speed of clouds and rain. The primal shapes of sky and clouds. The expanse of sky is slightly domed. Clouds appear to converge on a sunset in the pattern of a vortex.

Turner and Constable were the greatest painters of skies. This country and its continually changing weathers was their first inspiration. But what appears to be so effortlessly painted in their pictures was based on relentless observation.

LIGHT AND COLOUR

Light is a function of colour, and colour is a function of light. As we see form through light, there comes a time in painting when it is impossible to separate them. The Impressionist painters taught us to see colour in shadows. Chapter 4 deals with this. When you are actually in front of a landscape and painting, the colour of the shadows are often illusive. The theory of complementary colours in many cases does not even appear to 'work' in some landscapes. Always abandon any theory if the evidence of your own eyes disproves it. An infallible rule of light in colour, however, is the blueness of distances. As land recedes from the eye it loses its colour in blue. Misty days bring out blue in shadows.

Shadows in landscape are a problem. They give any structure, figure or still life, etc. its solidity. If you are painting the basic structural landscape like mountains, shadows will give them their solidity. But the shadows on mountains will change considerably from the morning till afternoon. In the south of Europe, shadows on mountains in sun, appear distinctly cobalt blue, so a painter like Cézanne was painting what he saw. When you are painting a landscape of a more intimate scale, the shadows are cast by, so to speak, things on the landscape, like trees and bushes.

This brings one on to the question of:

SCALE IN LANDSCAPE

This is something very subtle. Some stretches of landscape are large in scale, others small. Obviously, what gives a landscape its scale is the presence in some form or other of man, and his works. This brings back the point raised at the beginning of the chapter – that most landscape we now see bears unmistakably the evidence of man. Roads and pylons cross most landscapes. You have to decide, and this is an emotional decision, whether you accept them and paint them or not. Of course, if the painting looks better with motor cars and big roads, there is every reason for painting them in.

LANDSCAPE AND STRUCTURE

Two very different painters were interested in the basic structure of landscape, Leonardo da Vinci and Cézanne. The former was the founder of the High Renaissance in Italy, and the latter either one of the founders of modern painting or the last of the old masters, depending on how you interpret Cézanne. What is structure of landscape about? Leonardo saw it as the geological forms of the earth. To Cézanne the structure of landscape was part of his search for solid and enduring forms. There are kinds of landscape where the direct study of earth formation is essential – in certain sorts of mountain landscapes, or particularly unusual rocks. The final recommendation for studying this aspect of landscape is if you find it exciting and stimulating!

LANDSCAPE AND MOOD

To many people landscape in the sense of contemplating nature, is endlessly inspiring as we can then find a reflection of our moods. The forms and structures of a rolling well-cultivated landscape can bring a feeling of well-being. A fearful storm can make us feel awe. These are perfectly good starting points for the painter.

LANDSCAPE AND SEASONS

In the northern hemisphere, seasons in the landscape are clearly defined. They are marked by nature, and indeed by the hand of man. Pieter Breughel's marvellous series, *The Seasons* (that one cannot study enough), are about man in nature. A contemporary interpretation is worth trying. Perhaps we associate colours with seasons. This is reasonable enough.

OBSERVATIONS ON WINTER

The sun never rises very high and the sky will be at all

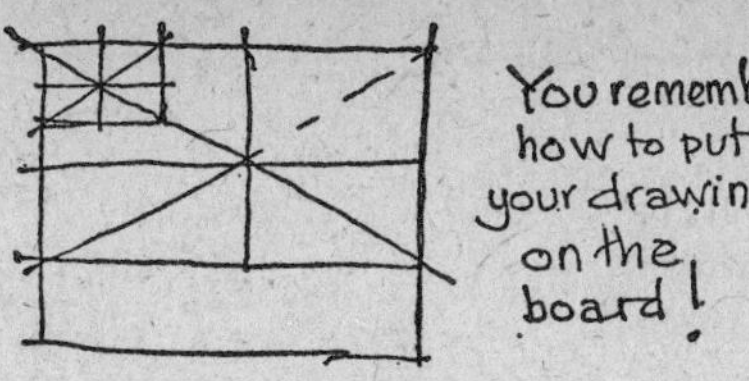

look for colours in shadows↓

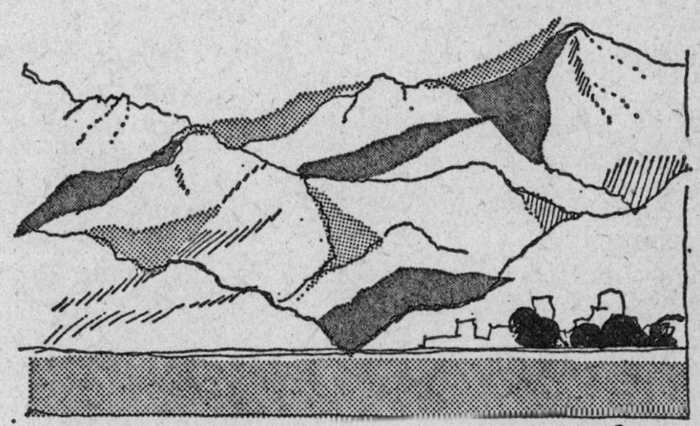

The shadows on mountains make you see solid form

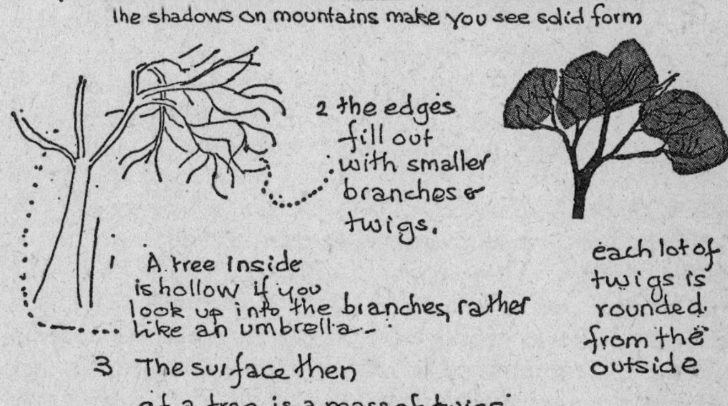

Fig. 40 Landscape painting.

times darker, and shadows longer. Winter is an excellent time to study the anatomy of trees. Remember, they are never, or at least very seldom, brown. Observe, in winter, the colours of the earth. Snow, of course, is delightful to paint, though like many unusual things in nature, snow-scapes have either to be painted very quickly or from sketches and memory. Snow is the classic representation of winter. It brings out the most beautiful silhouettes of trees and buildings, and everything else in the painting is tonally much darker than normal.

SPRING

Colours are unusually bright. It is worth enlarging your palette to get the true colours of clear bright greens. Take care when you are painting trees with blossom or new leaves, not to get the effect too spotty. This is avoided by taking the greatest care that the tones are in keeping with the whole painting. Skies are blue-green in March.

SUMMER

Most of one's landscape paintings are done in summer, for the very obvious reasons of longer days, holidays and the fact that one can get out more often because of warm weather. Most general observations on landscape presume that it is more or less summer. Your winter observations on bare landscape should be helpful in a summer landscape. The trees should be painted with care, seeing how leaves relate to the structure. This is just as true when they are in open landscape as in masses in forests (Fig. 40).

AUTUMN

If you have seen Impressionist paintings that were done when the Impressionists were in England, it is possible that the paintings must have been painted during the autumn, when, contrasted with leaves and the colour of light, you do see particularly strong blues in shadows. I never find the Impressionist theory 'works' in English landscape in the way it does in more southerly lights. In fact, the more one looks at British landscape the more one comes to see that Constable's eye was the most observant, when he saw that light and shadow are the unifying elements in our landscape.

PRACTICAL SUGGESTIONS

Keep your colours clear and clean at all times. Always think before adding white. Indiscriminate dipping into white can make colours dense and muddy.

For turquoise March-like skies use manganese blue and white.

For stormy skies and night, use the new permanent indigo.

To darken greens without using browns and blacks (which are drastic and will certainly turn to mud if white is then added): permanent green, being a mid green or viridian, can be darkened with violet, indigo, or ultramarine. All these will give cold darks. A commonly accepted definition of a cold colour is one that veers to blue; warm veers to red.

Greens can be neutralised, which is a way of giving a colour a half shadow by adding reds and oranges. This does not darken them overmuch and is exceedingly useful for shadows in distances. Neutral greens can also be made from blues and yellows, useful for the same reason.

Greens can be lightened and made warmer by adding yellow and yellow ochre. A very warm rich green can be mixed by adding orange to any green.

Yellows alone or mixed with white can be glazed with viridian or Winsor green to give very clear brilliant greens.

All the above notes on greens are relevant to northerly countries. In the Mediterranean, greens are mostly in the viridian and terre vert range.

ON PAINTING FROM LANDSCAPE

Paint in main areas of tone first (Fig. 41). The most popular colour for laying in is raw umber, though for landscape I find blue very good.

Decide on both the darkest area of the painting and the lightest, and paint these in first. Gradually build up the

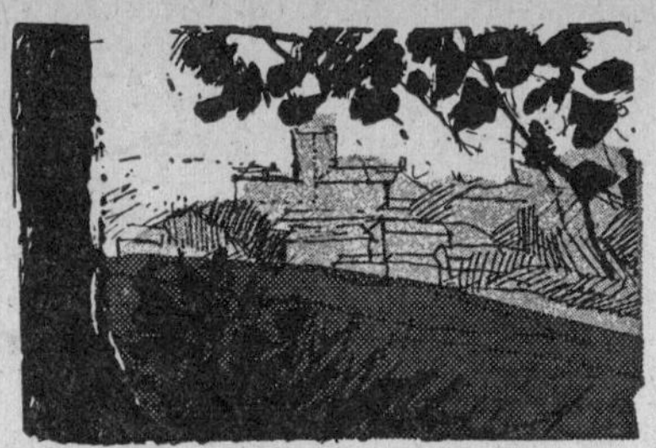

Fig. 41 Paint in shapes of main areas of tone first.

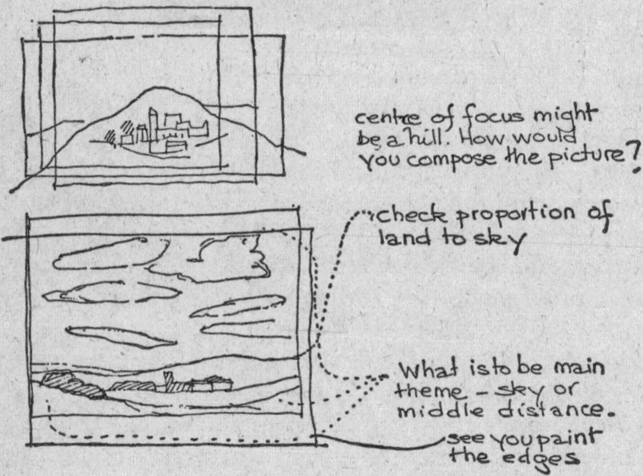

Fig. 42 Centres of focus.

other tones of colour. Avoid thinking of anything in the landscape as a detail to be kept till last, as this will lead to dislocation of tone. If it is the kind of day when clouds are moving rapidly, paint them in first with very quick brush strokes, using large brushes. Keep something in the view as a unit of measurement for scale. Factory chimneys are useful for this. Decide if anything in the landscape is to be centre of focusing. This is a problem of composition. Fig. 42 illustrates some obvious examples where there could be a centre of focus in landscape. Remember, these are only suggestions, and if you invent a way of painting landscape

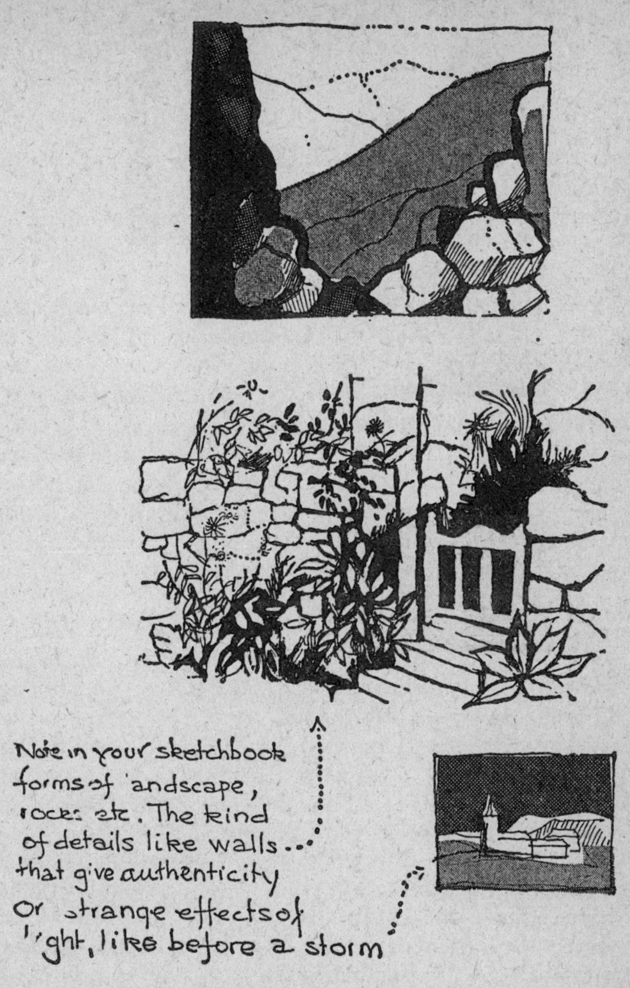

Fig. 43 Keeping a sketchbook.

that is more useful to you, then stick to it – providing that you are learning, enjoying yourself and, best of all, getting somewhere towards a good painting.

TRAINING YOUR EYES

Above all, landscape is about the observation of nature. One of the functions of a painter is to order our perception of the phenomena of nature. This can only be done by continual observation. So, to begin, here are some suggestions for ordering your observations:

Keep a sketch book by you. See how the countryside appears when you look into the light. Study the effect of weather on light; winds on colour. Curiously, winds do affect colour. Keep sketch book notes of details of landscape: natural details and man-made details (Fig. 43).

For small quick sketches, a board with a tinted ground is very useful. This has the middle tone ready for you, and it is only a question then of painting the lightest colours and the darkest. If possible, choose a tinted ground that is either warm or cold according to the light.

MOVE ABOUT CENTRE OF FOCUS

A landscape can also have a centre of focus, like a still life or even a portrait. An example of this is, say, in a painting of a farm, or a village on a hill. Here, your view finder described in the last chapter comes in useful to decide how much is going to be landscape, and how much the subject (Fig. 44). The more of landscape, the smaller the subject will appear. The same would be true if the subject were figures. You get a central point of focus in a landscape if you are painting a river going away from you (Fig. 44).

. . . Or an avenue of trees (Fig. 45).

It might be worth writing a few words about painting forests and trees. They are always a source of delight to look at, and most of us at some time or other have wished to paint a forest. The most obvious mess one usually gets in is to make the whole thing too spotty. This very easily happens with sun shining through trees, and is usually caused by

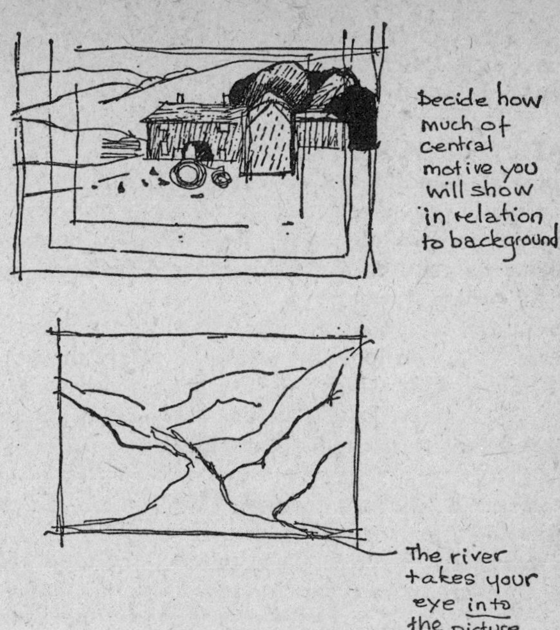

Fig. 44 The central point of focus.

stippling on the leaves at the end. When you are painting in a forest take careful note of the direction of the light. When the sun turns round so that the light has changed drastically, stop, or start another painting. The trunks and branches will be the unifying factor of the painting, and also give you something solid to build on. Branches, of course make for endless sources of patterns in the composition. Look very carefully for the actual colour of tree trunks. By tradition they are brown, though when you actually look, so many are shades of grey, and even green in damp places.

Make small paintings every so often of unusual colour effects. A bright colour in the distance or a dark distant colour in a landscape is always rather a problem, and it is worth experimenting to try to find a solution.

At the beginning of the chapter, I said that I would later

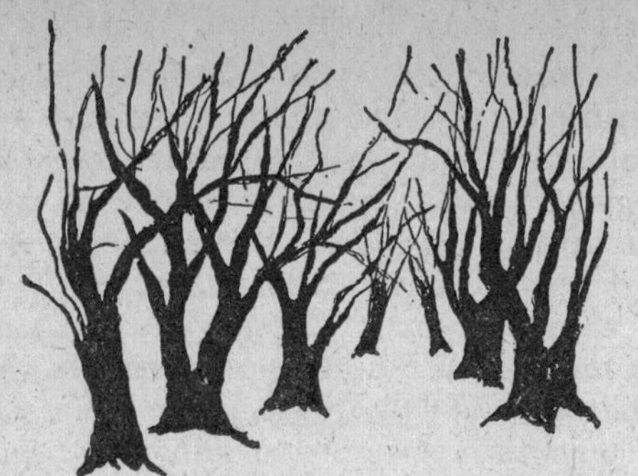

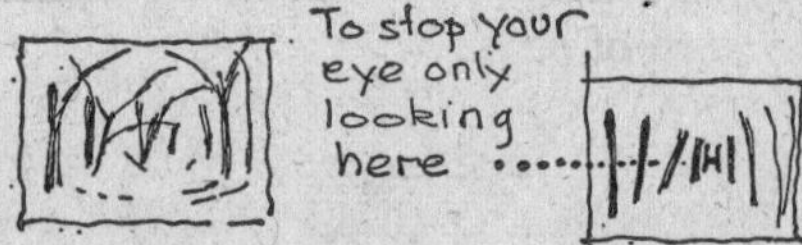

Fig. 45 Avenue of trees.

have something to say on abstraction in landscape, though this is almost a contradiction in itself. The rise of abstraction in the last sixty or so years, has coincided with the decline in landscape painting. Very few artists have painted abstractions from landscape. Abstraction is an urban vision of painting, which has nothing to do with the kind of relationship with nature essential to landscape painting. This is, however, no reason whatever for not painting landscape. If landscape is what you want to paint, never mind anything else, go ahead and paint, but there are difficulties in the very climate of the age in which we live. The meticulous observation that was natural to Constable, Breughel, and Cézanne as a boy in the countryside of his native Provence, is little valued in the general world view today. However, it is worth repeating that if the idea of painting landscapes brings back happy memories and gives you and other people pleasure, then abandon all doubts and start painting landscapes at once.

You could try doing abstracts from landscape. Gauguin, who appeared to paint from nature, quite obviously painted considerable parts of his works from imagination. As the whole is entirely consistent, this is a perfectly reasonable thing to do. Indeed, it is possible to paint a sort of landscape from imagination, with no direct reference to external nature, but this is dealt with in a later chapter. When all is said, the greatest of landscape painters have been chiefly interested in nature and philosophy. As Constable said, 'Why then may not landscape be considered as a branch of natural philosophy of which pictures are but experiments': Always be prepared to experiment with your painting. This may, on some occasions, lead to a painting turning out quite differently from your original intention, but this is the adventure of painting.

If at any time your painting has got into a hopeless muddle, stand back, take a good look. Decide whether a small detail is distracting the whole, check on tones and composition. When a painting is going badly, this is the time to be brave and go on; at these times it is worth being brave and making some experiments. Remember that a painting will look rather different in the indoors than when it is being painted in the open. If you find a landscape painting difficult to sort out, do not abandon it. Put the painting away for at least a month or so. Then come back to it afresh, and almost from a distance of time, the painting itself will tell you what to do.

It is possible to paint landscapes without direct reference to nature, and another chapter deals with this. Some painters' inner vision is so intense that it is difficult to tell from their paintings whether they saw with their vision or their eyes. This is so of two very different painters, Gauguin and Turner, where they may easily have put colours that they felt rather than saw. There is one rule there, that it was all consistent and right in terms of the painting.

You may find the following colour mixtures useful:

Indigo + *orange* gives a dark and neutral green.
Indigo + *yellow ochre* gives a dull neutral green that is slightly denser than the above mixture.

Raw umber + *cerulean* gives a neutral earth green.
Lemon yellow + *manganese blue* gives a spring green.

For cool greys use:

White + *indigo*.
White + *crimson* + *viridian*.
White + *black* is the absolute cold grey, but it is rather a lifeless colour and should be used with caution.

Warm greys are very useful in landscapes. You see them in rivers, clouds and even in earth:

White + *cobalt* + *light red*.
White + *purple* + *yellow ochre*.
White + *cerulean* + *cadmium red*.
White + *raw umber*.

All these colour combinations of greens and greys, can be used as mixture, or with the white as a base and the other colours glazed on top.

Reading over this chapter it appears that there are no definite rules for landscape painting. There cannot be, for what is a rule for one person is not helpful to another, and you must find what is your way.

There is one rule, however, that applies to every painter: Clean your equipment after the day's work!

The following painters well repay study, both for your instruction and enjoyment. If you cannot see them all in the galleries, then do so from picture books and colour slides.

Pieter Breughel. 1525–69. Flemish School.
Claude Lorraine. 1600–82. French-Roman School.
Nicolas Poussin. 1593–1665. French-Roman School.
Jacob van Ruysdael. 1628–82. Dutch School.
Peter Paul Rubens. 1577–1640. Flemish School.
John Crome. 1768–1821. British (Norwich) School.
J. M. W. Turner. 1775–1851. British School.
John Constable. 1776–1837. British School.

J. B. C. Corot. 1796–1875. French School.
Gustave Courbet. 1819–1877. French School.
Claude Monet. 1840–1926. French School.
Paul Cézanne. 1839–1906. French School.
Vincent Van Gogh. 1853–1890. Dutch School.
Paul Gauguin. 1839–1903. French School.

Now follows a list of actual paintings to see in Britain. While looking at the great names, also look out for the many delightful landscapes by obscure artists that you can see in museums. In some ways it is possible to feel more in common with a minor or even forgotten painter, who has distilled, on the surface of a painting, one moment of intense feeling.

A list of landscape paintings to look at in the British Isles, of course presents the embarrassment of choice. I hope that I have not left out anyone's favourite, and that the selection is reasonably fair. As with still life painting, always, in any gallery, look out for the unknown and the unexpected. The emphasis is not on any country or school though Dutch painters are well represented in this country, especially in Norwich.

Birmingham Museum and Art Gallery: J. D. Innes, *Provençal Coast.*

Bristol City Art Gallery: Courbet, *L'Eternité.*

Cardiff, National Museum of Wales: J. M. W. Turner, *Beacon light;* Cézanne, *Mountains in Provence;* Poussin, *Landscape With the Death of Phocion.*

Cambridge, Fitzwilliam Museum: Pieter Breughel, *Village Festival.*

Edinburgh, National Gallery: Claude, *Landscape With Fisherman and Angler;* Constable, *Vale of Dedham.*

Edinburgh, Museum of Modern Art: C. Permeke, *Winter in Flanders.*

Oxford, Ashmolean Museum: Claude, *Landscape With Ascanius and Stag;* Corot, *Landscape.*

Liverpool, Walker Art Gallery: Dughet, *Landscape With Pyramus and Thisbe;* Poussin, *Landscape With Figures.*

Manchester, City Art Gallery: J. D. Innes, *Welsh Mountain Landscape;* Constable, *A Cornfield.*
Newcastle, Laing Art Gallery: Constable, *Salisbury Cathedral from The Close;* Sheila Fell, *Landscape.*
Sheffield, Graves Art Gallery: R. Bevan, *Landscape With Farmhouse.*

The National Gallery, London, has of course many of the finest landscapes in the world. Of the many, look out for Rubens' most celebrated landscape painting, *The Château de Steen.* Also the magnificent works by Claude, Poussin, Ruysdael, Turner and Constable. The Cézanne landscapes are in the Courtauld Institute Galleries, London.

All the painters listed, and many others, can be studied from the series of excellent picture books published by Thames and Hudson and Phaidon Press.

OTHER USEFUL BOOKS

The Life of J. M. W. Turner by A. J. Finberg. Oxford University Press.

Drawing Trees by Colin Hayes. Studio Vista Publications.

Landscape Painting by John O'Conner. Studio Vista Publications.

Landscape Into Art by Kenneth Clark. John Murray.

TAILPIECE

Here are two very well known quotations, just in case you do not yet know them:

Poussin: 'Art is not a different thing from nature; nor can it pass beyond nature's boundaries. For that light of knowledge which by natural gift is scattered here and there and appears in different men in different times and places, is collected into one body by art.'

Cézanne: 'Treat nature by the cylinder, the sphere and the cone. Lines parallel to the horizon give breadth. Lines perpendicular to the horizon give depth.'

CHAPTER NINE

PAINTING A PORTRAIT

The last two years or so have seen a general revival of interest in the painted portrait. This is due to a great extent to the vision and enthusiasm of Dr Strong, Director of the National Portrait Gallery in London. The following quotation by Dr Strong from a catalogue of portrait paintings, is an excellent summing up of the position of today's portrait painter who, Dr Strong says, has 'a very special, intimate personal role. It (portraiture) alone can distil in a single static image the quintessential mood of a human being, those elements in a person that his friends and acquaintances evoke in the memory in his absence, and it is this alone which makes portraiture a viable form in the twentieth century.' In the past, before photography, a portrait told you what somebody looked like, or how the sitter wished everyone to see him, like a great Cardinal or Emperor. Portraiture is about the human image but equally, of course, it is about your board and paint. And this is where we must begin.

At first, the idea of doing a portrait is rather formidable. However, many of the difficulties are really non-existent when you think about it. Especially the problem of likeness. It is true that some painters do have a curious facility for depicting likeness, but if you have not, you can soon learn how. One of the first requirements for a beginner in portrait painting, is to feel at ease with the subject. If you are in a group or on your own with a professional model, the model will not make, even unintentionally, a demolishing remark about your work. If you have not got or cannot afford endless sessions with a professional model, you must have an understanding and willing subject, so that if anything does go wrong they will not mind too much. Of course, the more

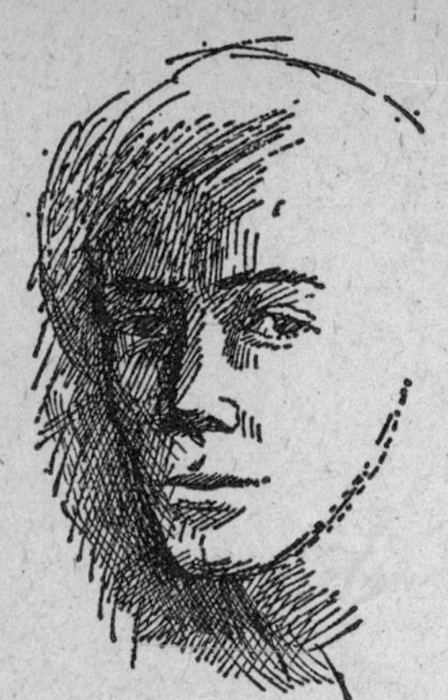

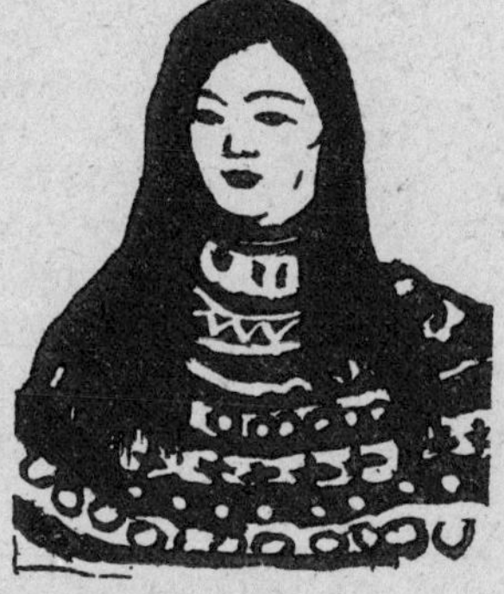

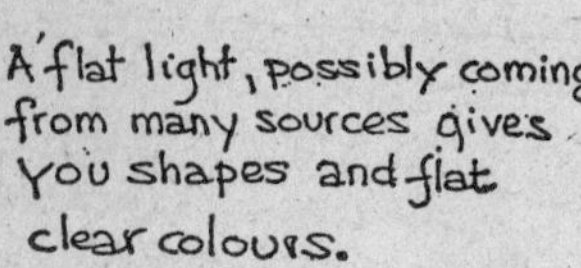

Fig. 46 Lighting a portrait.

at ease you are with a sitter the less likely it is the portrait will go wrong. Explain to the sitter at the beginning, that you may need more sessions of work than you thought.

MAKING A BEGINNING

Your subject must be in a constant light, and it is worth experimenting with light to find out the kind that appeals to you the most (Fig. 46).

As well as being in a constant light the sitter should be in a comfortable position. Remember that the way people sit, and the characteristic way they hold their heads, are an integral part of portraiture and likeness. Naturally at each portrait sitting, the subject should return to the very same position and lighting.

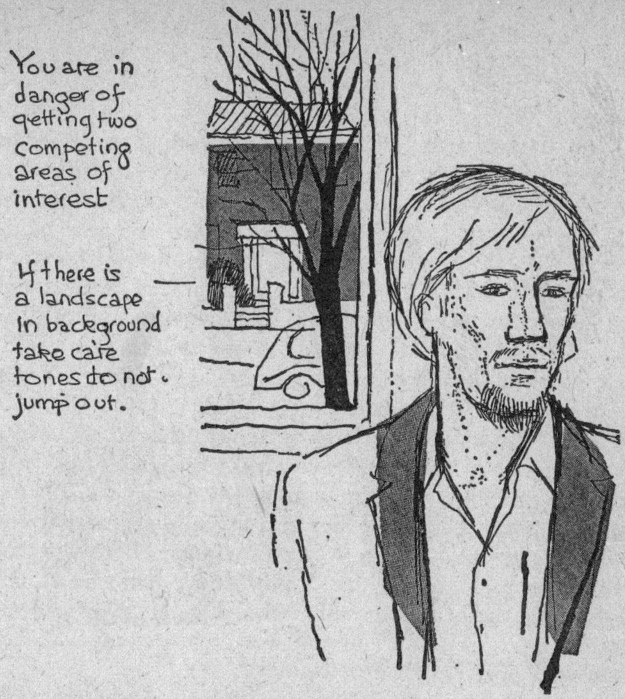

Fig. 47 Background.

BACKGROUNDS

Some painters drape the background with cloth over screens in a colour that will suit the model's complexion and clothing. It is very agreeable to experiment with colours and patterns in this way. The old masters used to paint backgrounds suitable to the subject, even a grand vista of a landscape. Choose any background, but if it has a complicated pattern or detailed view, take care that you do not get the problem of a painting that has two opposing interests (Fig. 47). Many contemporary painters do not contrive a background at all, and paint the incidentals of the studio just as they are. If there were a rule to go by, a reasonable one might be to see that the background enhances the sitter's complexion.

PAINTING

If you have done the drawings for portraiture suggested in Chapter 7 you are ready to begin. Transfer the drawing that is most suitable to the board. Many artists like to sketch in with charcoal but you might as well start with the paint directly. Use any colour, though raw umber is the most popular. However attractive the preliminary drawing in raw umber may look, you should be brave and start adding colour. Cover the whole area of the board with paint, with large brushes. Do not be carried away at the beginning of a painting with the head, hoping to 'catch up' on the rest later; this never works. Make quite sure that all the areas of the board are covered, leaving no white of the priming showing through, as this can completely distort the colours. Once the board is covered then you can start to build up the head. At this stage, do not worry overmuch about whether eyes, nose and mouth are 'right'. For, looking at the anatomy of the head from all angles (Fig. 48), you will see that the eyes, nose and mouth are only a comparatively small area of the cranium.

Concentrate for now on building up the mass of the head.

Flesh Colours. To some people, the idea of mixing flesh colours is an alarming prospect. But, it need not be, providing you keep your colours clean. When Gauguin painted his beautiful Tahitan women, it is obvious that he used yellow ochre as the base for painting a dark skin. The yellow ochre was then mixed with light reds, raw umbers, viridians, and even some ultramarine in the shadows. In painting a dark skin the whole tonal range is very low, and even the highest lighted parts of the skin are dark in relation to white. In painting a dark skin, take care not to add too much white at any time, as this can make colour chalky and dull. For a dark skin you can use backgrounds of very brilliant colours and patterns. The tonal range of the flesh colours balance them.

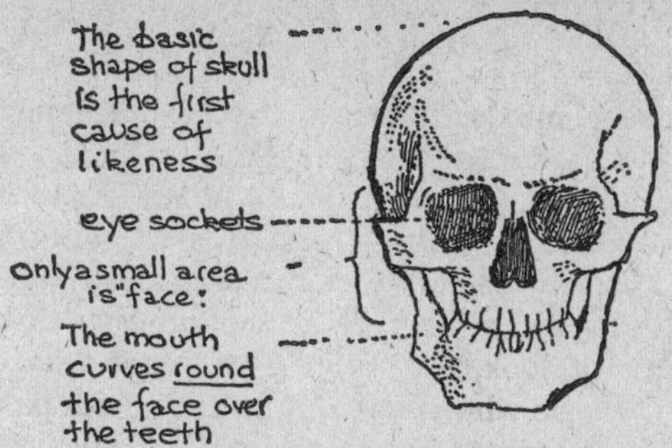

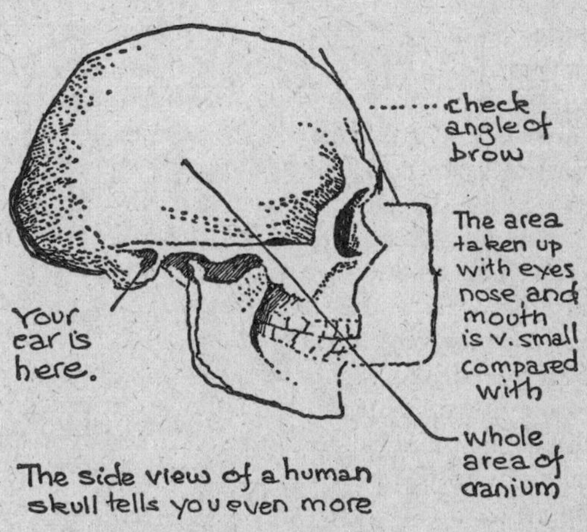

Fig. 48 Anatomy of the head.

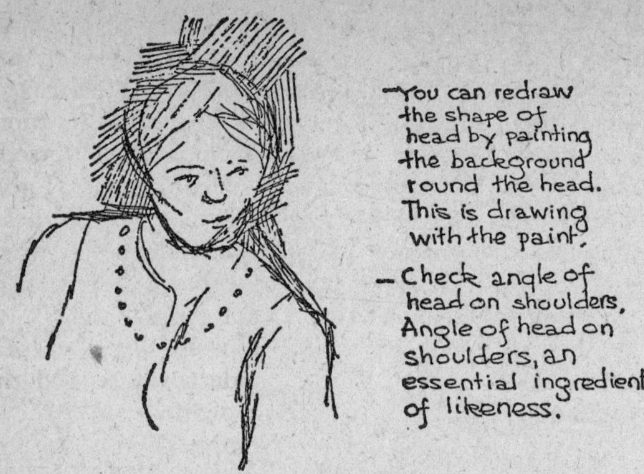

Fig. 49 Checking the outline shape of the head.

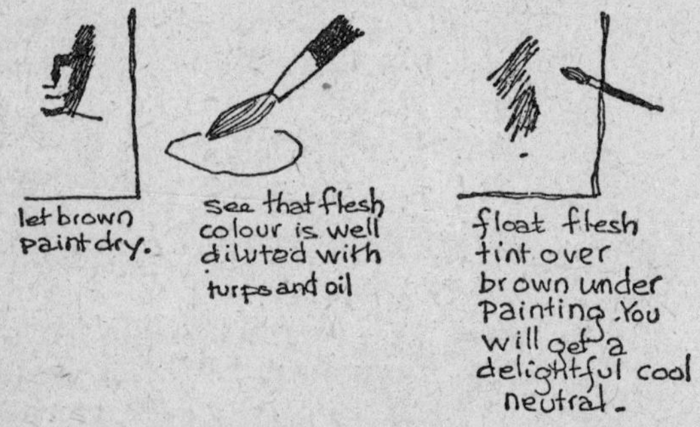

Fig. 50 Shadows.

A European skin needs a basis of white paint. Start with white. Then add some yellow ochre, to colour the white slightly. You can then add a touch of either light red or cadmium red. The result will be a basic flesh tint, that can be varied in the proportions of these three colours. Over the surface of the face there are a great number of very subtle changes of tone and colour. So, to start, mix a colour that is more or less the middle colour and to tone. Cover the whole area of the head. Then the colour of the amount of hair that is showing. Re-check the outline shape of the head (Fig. 49). Draw with the background colour if it needs alteration. This is an example where drawing and painting intersect, and cannot be separated. As in still life, shadow will give mass and form to the head. Painting shadows to the head has to be treated with care. If you had laid the original design in with raw umber, or light red, then a thin layer of the flesh colour over them gives a cool grey shadow. This was a method used by Rubens, Gainsborough, and all their contemporaries. Renoir, in more modern times used the same technique (Fig. 50). This method of obtaining shadows gives only a delicate shadow. To get a more decisive shadow the following mixtures are useful: a red based flesh colour can be neutralised to give a shadow of medium depth by the addition of blues and greens. For really dark shadows, it is equally important to keep the shadows clean. One can use raw umbers and other browns and greens for shadows. This was done by the old masters. If you are looking for colours in shadows, the following mixtures have greater range.

Yellow ochre + raw umber: for a warm based shadow.

Green + orange: for a very rich shadow, useful on dark skins.

Raw umber + purple + light red: for an unusual and rather cold shadow.

Light red + dark green: for a deep rich shadow.

The flesh tint sold in tubes while rather insensitive for the highlights of flesh, is useful for mixing with greens, raw umber, yellow ochre and light red to lighten the tone for a medium shadow. Impressionist portraits, and those of Cézanne, distinctly show complementary colours in shadows. If you see them, paint them, but as in landscape, always abandon a theory if it doesn't work. On the surface of a head, especially in the intricacies of an aged head, you can frequently see a combination of cold and warm shadows.

By now, you should have laid in the main areas of the head, light and shadow, as shown in Fig. 51.

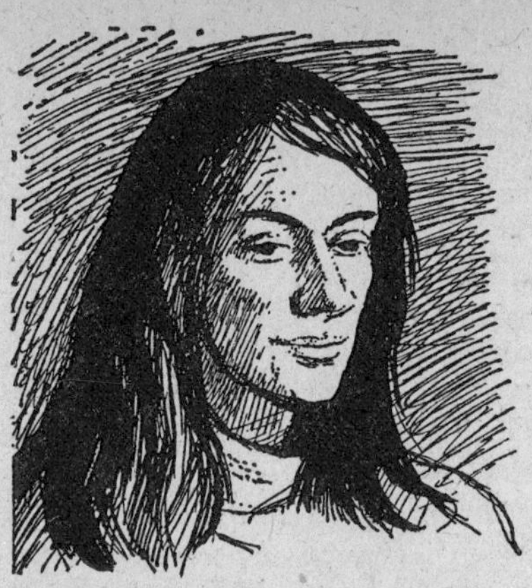

Fig. 51 Light and shadows.

Before you get carried away too far (as one can painting a head) put more paint on other parts of the board. Keep the density of the paint on the board more or less even. Do not let one part get overpainted. The tones of clothing or colours may need adjusting. If one colour looks wrong, re-work on it but also check that the colour next to it is working too. In any painting, you cannot paint on any colour without it affecting all the others.

Coming back to work on the head, it will now be necessary to break down the head to its details. This does not mean immediately the addition of eyelashes and wrinkles. It is as well to check up again on proportions; this is a detail too.

Look carefully at the tonality of the shadows round the nose and the eye sockets, as well as the colour of the shadows. Paint in the shapes of the eye sockets and nose. You will now see what we generally mean by a face forming itself. Then do the same for the line of the jaw. Continually measure proportion, but now more intricately. It is in fact possible to build up a head purely by marks of measuring proportion (Fig. 52). A painting by Sir William Coldstream is built up in this way. It means, that if you have no natural flair for

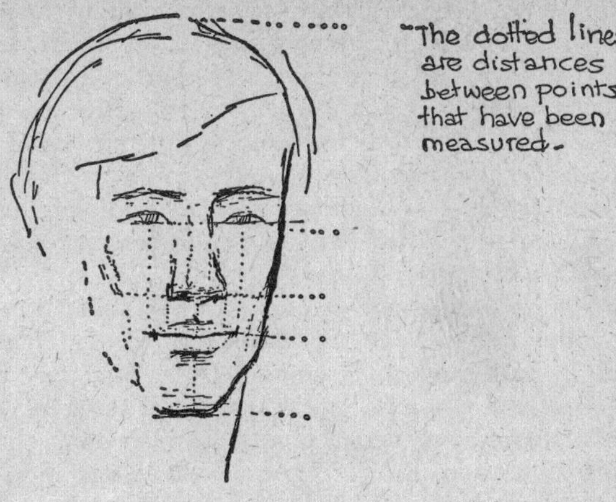

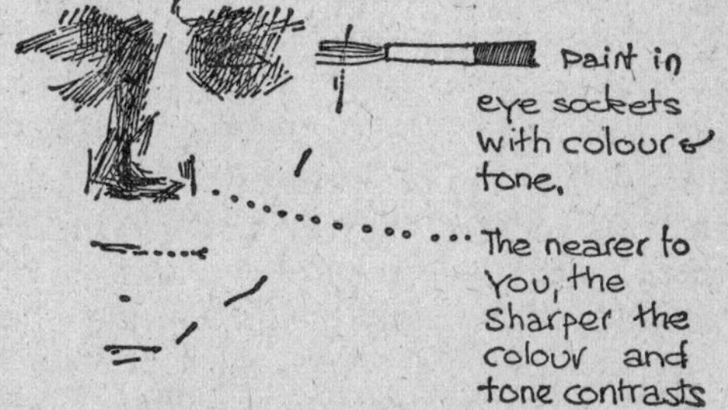

Fig. 52 Measuring proportion and filling in detail.

'likeness', by accurate measurement you can arrive at the same result.

After more work on the head go back to painting the rest of the picture. By now, you may find that the hands need some intensive work on them. Hands are part of a person's character; consider their shape and size. Do not be put off by the superstition that drawing hands is difficult. Think of hands shape for shape as in Fig. 53, and as a tool for grasping things. Before you know where you are, you will have painted a hand and learned more about the very subtle closeness of painting and drawing.

When you are struggling with a portrait, it can be dreadfully discouraging to hear the classic criticism: 'There's something wrong with the mouth.' It is true that the subtlest change of emphasis can make all the difference to the finer points of expression, as in a strip-cartoon, where the merest alteration of a line gives a whole variation of expressions to a face. However, before we become too involved in that, it is worth considering the structure of eyes and mouth in detail (Fig. 54). Some beginners paint the eyes and mouth flat on the face, without really looking. When Cézanne painted his self portraits, he was concerned with the problems of solid form in terms of colour. It is this that gives his self portraits their austere nobility. This is, of course, a perfectly reasonable approach to portraiture, if it appeals to you. However, if you are interested in the subtleties of expression, you will know that it is a problem that has fascinated most portrait painters since the invention of oil paint.

EXPRESSION

Franz Hals and Rubens, had the northern painters' characteristic of a fascination with light on surface. To look at their brilliant portraits it appears that they capture the fleeting expression by the highlights on the head. To an extent this is true. Some painters have a quite natural flair for swift and bright brush strokes that can capture a fleeting expression. The way to practise this, if you want to, is by

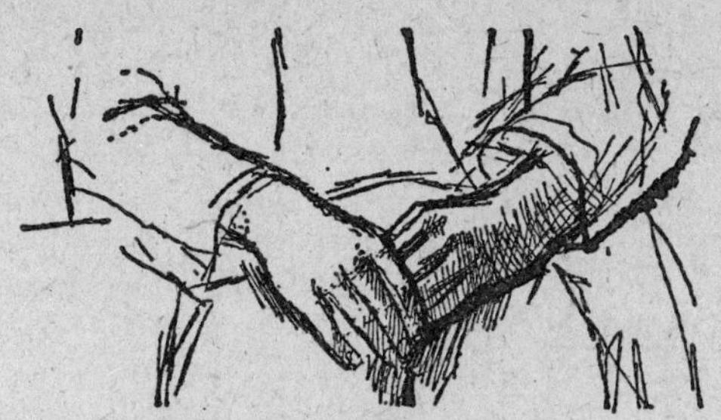

hands are a major part of likeness. Not as formidable to paint and draw as all that. Think of an instrument to pick things up; then you will understand how a hand works

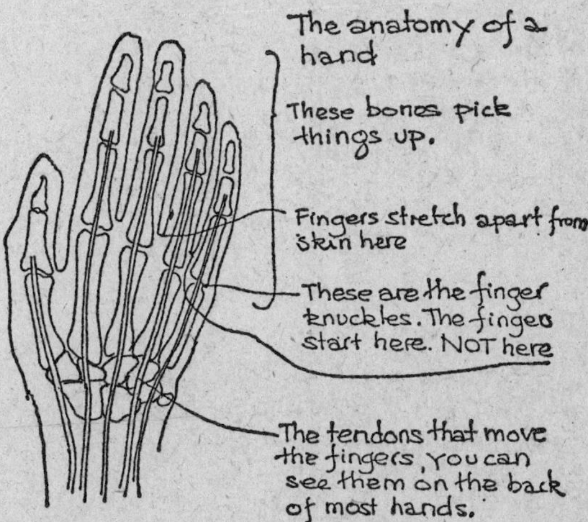

Fig. 53 Hands.

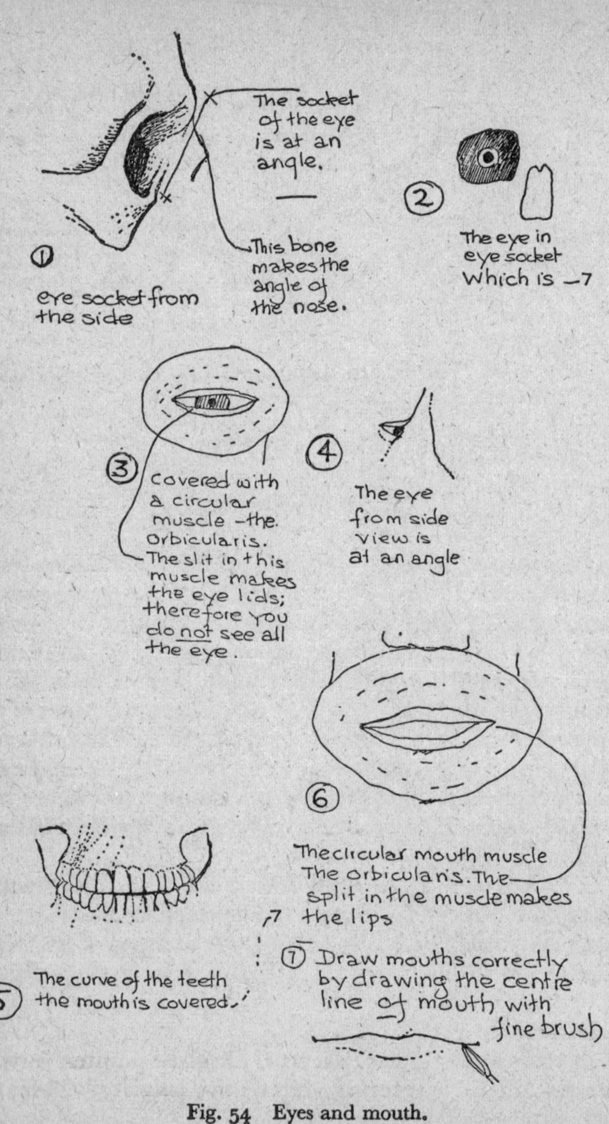

Fig. 54 Eyes and mouth.

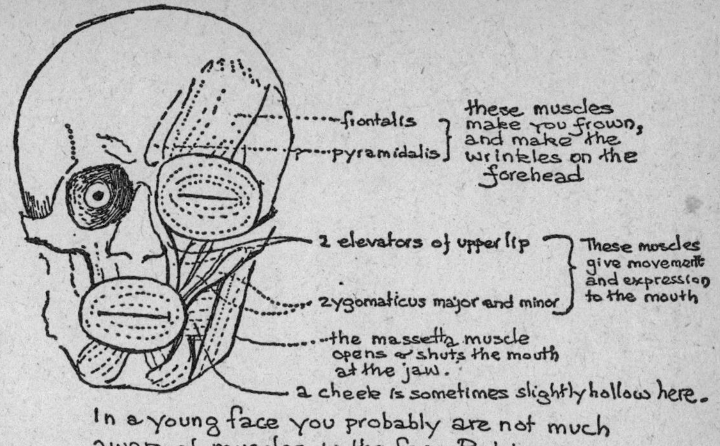

Fig. 55 Facial muscles.

painting many quick portraits in very fluid paint. Expression is not, however, only a question of 'catching' it by chance. Expression on the human head is conditioned by muscles. It is these muscles that make the wrinkles on an old person's head (Fig. 55). So expression must also be part of the structure of the head. The most marvellous examples of this are in Rembrandt's self portraits in his old age. The structure of the head, the expression, and the paint are in perfect unity. Study a Rembrandt and a Velasquez too, to see how the paint is handled in such a way that we 'read' wrinkles or smiles.

To come back to the main area of the head. Hair is something that can get out of tone. Always look for hair following the main structure of the head. Look at types of hair: hair that sits firmly on the skull, or hangs in locks (Fig. 56).

LIKENESS

Is there a mystique of likeness? Do some painters have an innate gift for capturing this elusive quality? These are

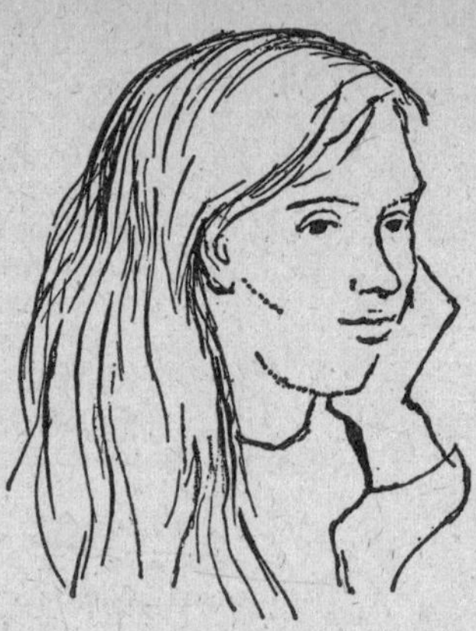

Fig. 56 Paint and draw hair following contours of the skull. See how shape of skull affects hair growth.

questions I have often heard asked, and there is a possible explanation. Clearly, some painters have a sense of relevant information. This is a sense that is given to great painters, writers and scientists, but especially painters and scientists. They have an instinct, or what you will, to seek out in the natural world the pulse or the central core of things. One feels in looking at a great portrait, that the painter has sensed what are the most relevant expressions and main structures of his subject. Not that this is always a gift that you either have or have not. By continual observation and work, it can be acquired. It is a curious fact, that, with the possible exception of Hals, great portrait painters could also paint marvellous pictures of anything else, though, there have been masters of the still life and landscape who could do that alone. If, then, portrait painting appeals to you, everything else you paint will help it.

PAINTING CHILDREN

This is perhaps a special branch of portraiture where the above rule does not entirely apply. Painting children does

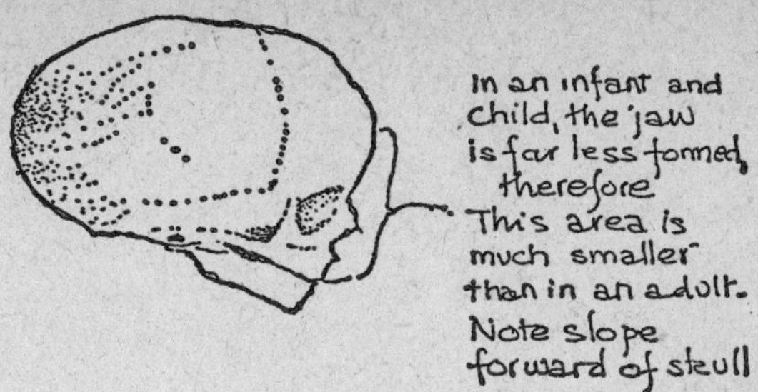

Fig. 57 An infant's skull.

need a special comment to itself, for it needs, above everything else, a very special relationship with the child. Sittings have to be shorter. Children's skins are particularly delicate and clear, and your flesh tints have to be clear accordingly. The best children's portraits are obviously done very quickly and spontaneously.

Of course, a child's head receives its character from the very fact that its bones are less formed, and its features less definite (Fig. 57). Children have very swift changes ot expression and mood. There is no branch of painting that gives more pleasure to others than that of a sensitive portraif of a child.

Constable's observation that landscape was a branch of natural philosophy (science as we understand it today) can equally apply to portraiture. Through portraits, we can look back at the past, and see what will always be constant in people at all times. In painting a portrait, one not only learns more about the visual forms that are eternal, but also more about mankind and ourselves. If you always look for the constants in any branch of painting, this is the way you will approach toward a truthful portrait. Some people believe that if you try to make a portrait as cruel and as nasty as possible, it is 'truer' than if you had not.

To revert to the ugly and disgusting in painting, can be taken as an open admission of complete emptiness, since one has obviously had to draw attention to oneself somehow. But to revert to the problem of a true likeness. Many persons, when discussing a portrait, raise the question of photography. This leads to all kinds of arguments that, thank goodness, there is no room for here. What is more relevant, is whether one can use photographs as helps in painting. Simply, if you find them helpful, do so. Do be warned, however, against imitating in so versatile a medium as oil paint, the smooth and shiny surface of a photograph.

SOME MORE COLOUR MIXTURES AND SUGGESTIONS TO FINISH THE CHAPTER

For the delicate texture of cheeks. With a very fair flesh colour, like a child's, can have a white and lemon yellow base, with additions of reds.

The beautiful oriental skins, have a base of mostly yellow ochre and white, with a touch of orange to make the colour warmer.

Cobalt violet into a basic flesh colour mixture gives a warm, not too dark, shadow.

A few more words about backgrounds: A background colour can be used to bring out the colour of skin. Warm-toned skins, and cold-toned skins, can have backgrounds of colours that either enhance or play down these characteristics.

Many painters always like to have a vertical or a horizontal in a portrait by which to measure everything else.

PAINTERS TO LOOK AT, IN BOOKS, SLIDES OR REALITY

Raphael, 1483–1520. Italian School.
Titian, 1487–1576. Venetian School.
Jan Van Eyck, fl. 1422–41. Flemish School.
El Greco, 1541–1614. Spanish School.
Peter Paul Rubens, 1577–1640. Flemish School.
Velasquez, 1599–1660. Spanish School.
Franz Hals, 1580–1666. Dutch School.
Rembrandt, 1606–69. Dutch School.

Boucher, 1703–70. French School.
Goya, 1746–1828. Spanish School.
Ingres, 1780–1867. French School.
Delacroix, 1798–1863. French School.
Courbet, 1819–1877. French School.
Degas, 1834–1917. French School.
Cézanne, 1839–1906. French School.
Picasso (Blue and Rose periods) 1881–

Plus, of course, the founder of our tradition in portraiture, one of the greatest, Hans Holbein the younger, 1497–1543, who was born in Basle, but spent many years in England during the reign of Henry VIII.

There are many very excellent portraits in the British Isles. It has been difficult to make a selection, and you may choose quite different ones. Those selected have been chosen as examples of painting, and as representative of their times. A good portrait tells you about painting, the person, something of the artist's personality, and the age in which he lived.

Cambridge, Fitzwilliam Museum: Franz Hals, *Portrait of a Man*.

Birmingham, Museum and Art Gallery: Graham Sutherland, *Portrait of the Hon. Edward Sackville-West;* Subleyras, *Portrait of St. John of Avila*.

Edinburgh, National Gallery of Scotland: Raeburn, *McDonnel of Glengarry*.

Glasgow, Art Gallery: Rembrandt, *A Man in Armour*.

Liverpool, Walker Art Gallery: Rembrandt, *Self Portrait when Young*.

Newcastle, Laing Art Gallery: A. John, *Two Gitanes*.

London, National Gallery: Titian, *Portrait of a Man in Blue;* A. del Sarto, *Portrait of a Sculptor*. Among several magnificent van Dycks there is the *Charles I on Horseback*. The National Gallery has several great Rembrandt portraits and self portraits, all of course are worthy of study.

Velasquez, *Portrait of Philip IV as a Young Man;* Goya, *Portrait of Dona Isabel Cobos;* Gainsborough, *Portrait of Sarah Siddons;* Cézanne, *Self Portrait.*

You probably do not need to be reminded of the absorbing collection of portraits in the National Portrait Gallery, London. Or, equally, the Scottish National Portrait Gallery in Edinburgh.

Local museums and stately homes in England often have fine portraits by the Elizabethans, also Reynolds, Gainsborough, Lawrence, etc. Unfortunately in England, we do not see so much of the two splendid Scottish painters Raeburn and Ramsay, who well repay any amount of study.

BOOKS FOR FURTHER STUDY

Painting Children by Benedict Rubbra. Studio Vista.

Starting to Paint Portraits by Bernard Dunstan, R.A. Studio Vista.

Thames and Hudson and Phaidon Press publish excellent picture books on the artists listed.

CHAPTER TEN

THE FIGURE

The first part of this chapter is about painting from the figure, directly in the same way as a landscape or still life. This, of course, presents the problem of a model. The answer to this is to share one with a group of friends, or join a group or class. Naturally, you could employ a model all to yourself, but it is expensive. It is not conducive to relaxed painting to feel that everything that goes wrong is also wasting money!

Before we get much further, I must begin with a sort of apologia. The nude figure, I believe, is primarily an object of delight and pleasure to look at. For many years, in our art schools and exhibitions, the nude has been treated rather differently. The nude was inclined to be posed against rather sad backgrounds of radiators and platforms. In exhibitions most paintings that included the nude, presented the model justified in some way. She was lying down on a bed, or dressing, or washing. This may have been due to the very forceful personality of Sickert on British art. Of course, it is perfectly good to paint the nude in this way, though I have to admit to a strong bias to the nude in the classical tradition as exemplified by the beautiful and sensual nudes of Giorgione and Titian, Veronese, Velasquez, Boucher and, latterly, Gauguin and Modigliani. Not that the classic nude is any the easier to paint; beautiful and noble forms are always the most difficult. When you have tried painting the nude, you will see why, by tradition, it has always been considered one of the greatest tests of an artist's ability.

The chapter on drawing did not mention drawing from life. Life drawing is difficult, and one cannot pretend it is easy. However, it is worth remembering that it is one branch of drawing where some persons excel, who yet do not or cannot paint. So, like all other kinds of painting the idea is to keep drawing and painting as close as possible. Chapter 7 *did* deal with volume and rhythm; and these are good enough starting points for the nude.

When posing the model, comfortable and natural positions are essential (Fig. 58). Otherwise the finished result will never look right. Begin with a few drawings to sort out what you are going to paint. Before we start, however, study the diagram of basic anatomy (Fig. 59). The bones give the volume and rhythm, the backbone gives the basic rhythm of the body so, with an idea about volume and rhythm, you can start drawing. Proportion is important too. Some people have a natural eye for proportion. If not, measuring is just as good. A good idea is to take something within the area of vision as the norm of proportion by which everything else is measured.

PAINTING

The formulae for flesh colours in the last chapter on portraiture are just as good for the nude as for portraits, though, in general, the colour of body flesh is lighter in tone. You might like to take the idea of glazing flesh colours further. This is a method of painting skin used to marvellous effect by Rubens and Renoir. For a fair skin, on a ground of lemon yellow, yellow ochre and white, glaze, with paint mixed to transparency in oil and turpentine; this will give a transparent flesh tint.

Looking at the nude, parts of the body vary considerably in colour, and therefore in tonality. Unity is preserved in the drawing, or even better expressed by the French word *dessin*. Also, you should choose a colour and tone that is the one of the largest area to paint of the whole of the body. This will also give the body unity. As in every other painting, the whole area should be worked on together. Many painters of the nude like a white next to the model. This is in fact useful, as it shows that the lightest skin is several colour tones darker than the white paint (Fig. 61).

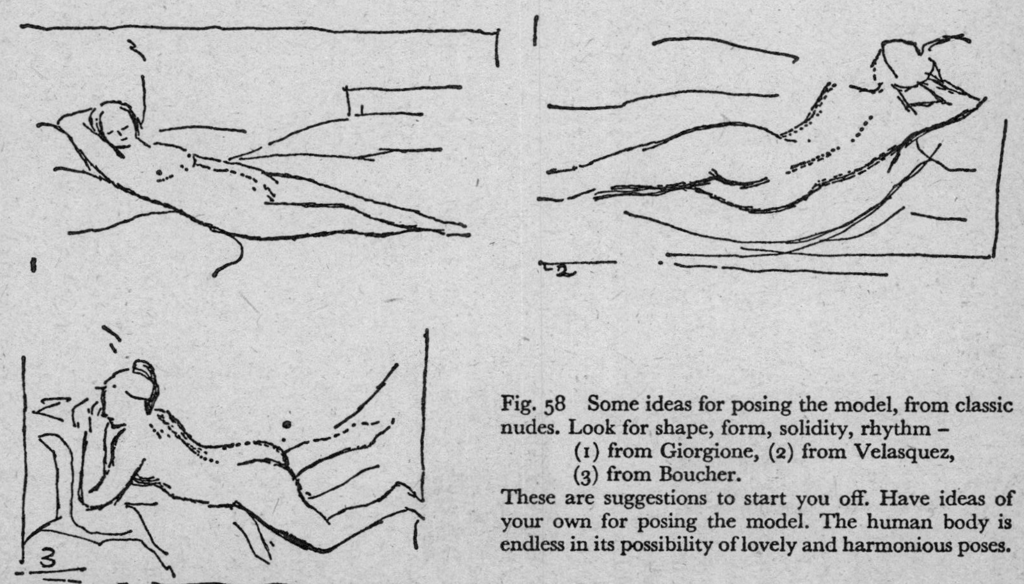

Fig. 58 Some ideas for posing the model, from classic nudes. Look for shape, form, solidity, rhythm –
(1) from Giorgione, (2) from Velasquez,
(3) from Boucher.

These are suggestions to start you off. Have ideas of your own for posing the model. The human body is endless in its possibility of lovely and harmonious poses.

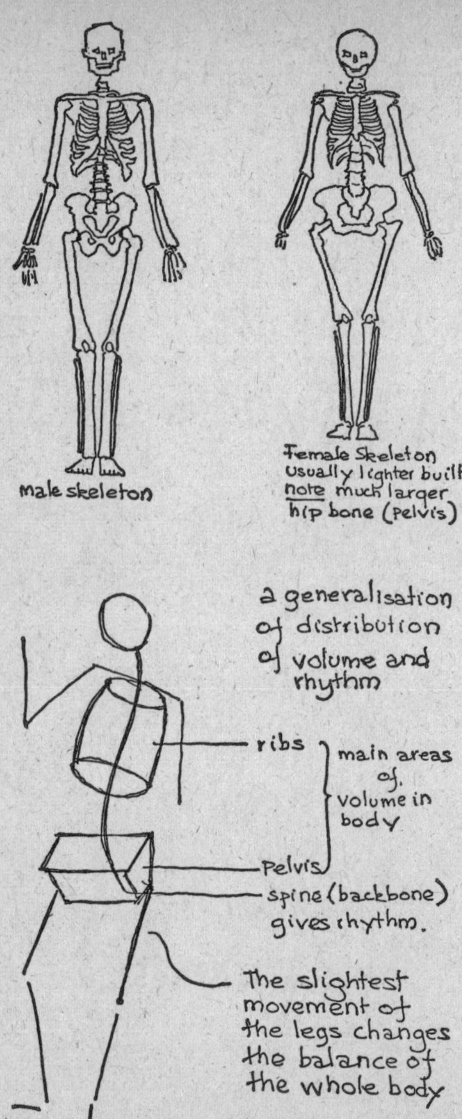

Fig. 59 Basic anatomy.

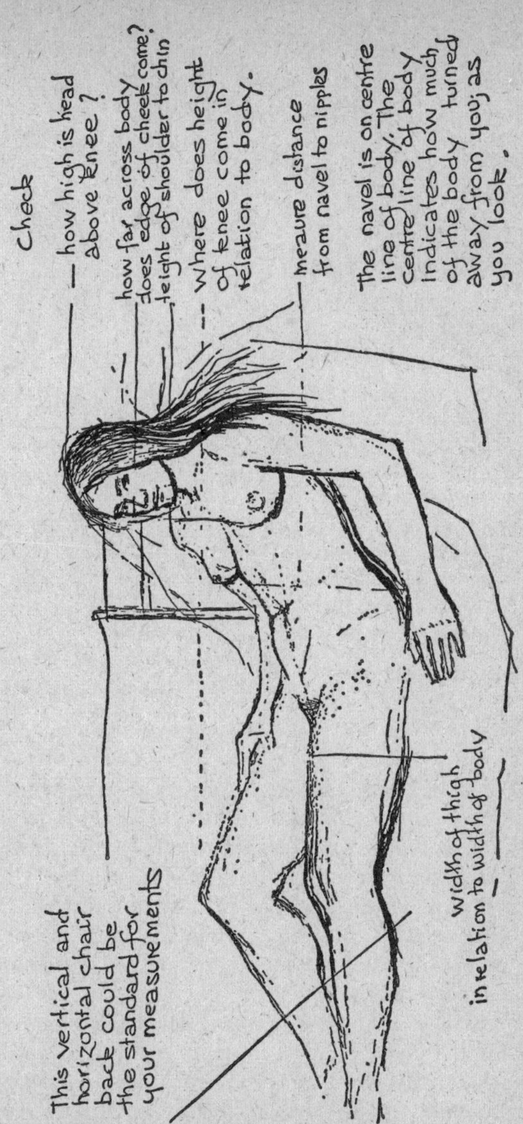

Fig. 60 Proportion.

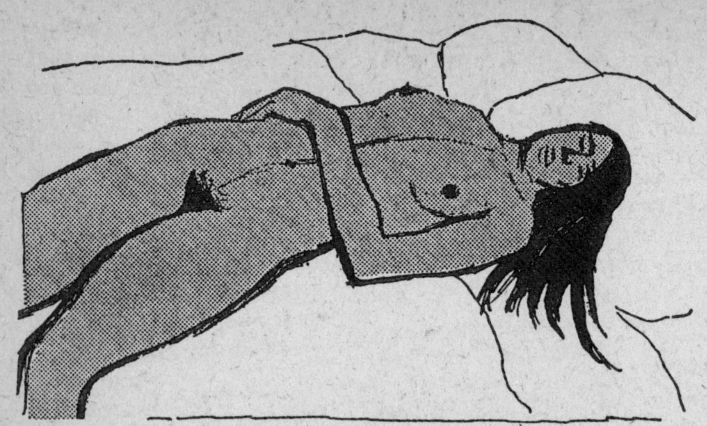

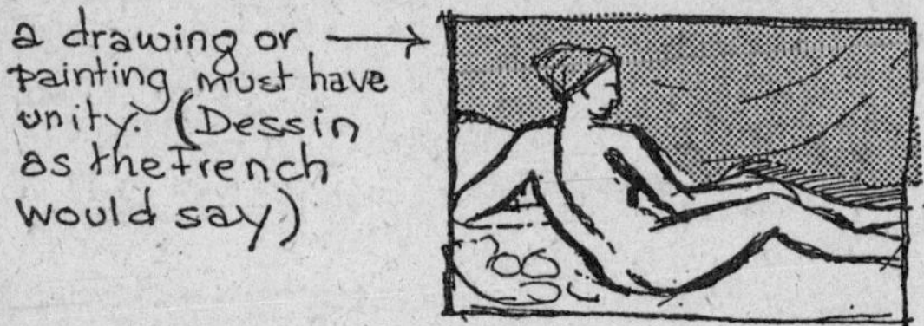

Fig. 61 Unity and tone.

The human body contains hundreds of subtle movements and planes. Any one area of the body appears to have an infinity of colours. One should try to paint these subtle changes in colour as well as painting the unity of the body. However, this is more easily written than painted. The very fact that one's life painting, when finished, falls short of what one wished, is, strangely, the thing that makes one want to try the next.

As models come in sessions, the times in between are useful for taking stock, and looking at the painting. If you can work on the painting away from the model this helps bring the painting together. Painting from direct nature can even confuse one, with so much to get on canvas. The one thing that usually ruins a life painting, apart from bad drawing, is disagreeable colour. The subtleties of flesh are difficult, but the secret of painting good colour is clarity. The more one mixes up colours hoping the mixing will yield something new, the worse it gets. The reason is that dense mixtures on a ground prevent the reflection of light. Many painters get into hopeless muddles mixing away on their palette hoping to get colour exactly right. The fact is, that the colours on your palette are never exactly like those in external nature. All you can get is a workable approximation that is right in terms of the painting. To get clear flesh colours, mix as simply as possible. If the colours you use are not enough, get some more and experiment.

SOME MORE ABOUT MIXING FLESH COLOURS USING NO MORE THAN THREE COLOURS

White + a touch of orange + a touch of violet: gives an unusual variation of flesh colour.

Viridian + crimson or rose: gives a sensitive neutral for shadows.

White + a touch of orange + a touch of cobalt: gives a light-toned neutral for subtle shadows.

White + raw umber + rose or crimson: gives a neutral light-purplish tint.

SHADOWS

The same applies to nudes as to portraits. On the expanse of flesh, it is possible – slightly more so than in a portrait – to distinguish between a 'cold' light and a 'warm' light. Some painting manuals say that in a warm light you find cool colours, and the other way about. This, in terms of actual colour is more or less the idea of complementary colours. Once you know about complementary colours, you will see them, having been told. However every time a theory is refuted by the evidence of your eyes, then it is not for you. Titian and Giorgione apparently obtained the modulations

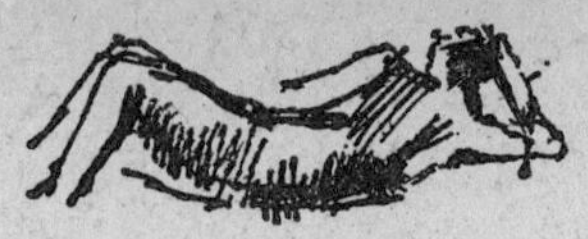

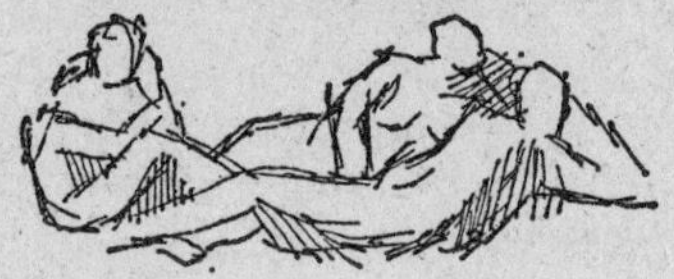

Fig. 62 We can see in landscape and the human form:– rhythm, undulations, hills, valleys, volumes. Some landscapes are rounded and abundant like a nude.

on their beautiful nudes by glazing on transparent darks. This, of course, gives clear shadows. The underpainting should dry a bit before glazing on top. If a painting is in a complete impasse, do not worry. The one cure is ruthlessly to take out with a palette knife the parts that are ruining the rest. Then boldly repaint. This will not do the painting any harm. A painting is a living thing. It has a seed of an idea which grows. Sometimes it needs grafts and some drastic pruning too. What is more likely to kill a painting is going over and over repeating the same parts. You can go on working and experimenting on a painting until you almost lose physical contact with the paint. Then the painting is finished.

It is certain that if you have produced a marvellous painting of the nude you could paint anything else. So consider for a moment where the nude relates to other kinds of painting. One of my first teachers, who remembers Paris in the 1900s, repeated this attractive story about Renoir: that he painted soft, dainty flowers and fruits as a form of practice for his nudes. True or not, there is a distinct similarity of treatment between the subjects. Renoir did, in fact, once write that one should 'caress the canvas with the

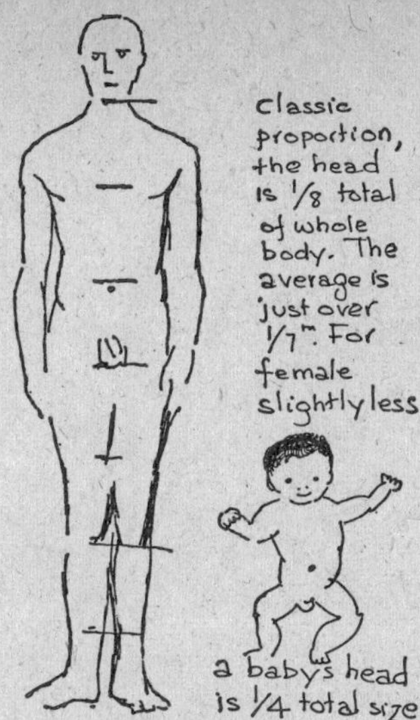

Fig. 63 Figure proportion.

brush'. Of course Renoir's marvellous transparent colours were made possible by the hot climate where he painted. This meant that paint dried very quickly, and one could build up transparent layers like a water colour – a thought to bear in mind if you ever go to paint in the south, or warm countries. Many artists must, unconsciously, have realised the relationship between the figure and forms of landscape. Henry Moore, the sculptor, directly relates his figures to landscape. Painters could do so. There are landscapes with rounded and undulating forms that many remarks on painting the nude could apply to as well (Fig. 62). The great Italian painters believed that the beautiful nude human form depended on proportion. This meant 'ideal' proportion, a conception that was also evolved in architecture. If you find you respond to the idea of an ideally proportioned body, by all means experiment. This attitude to proportion differs from that mentioned earlier which

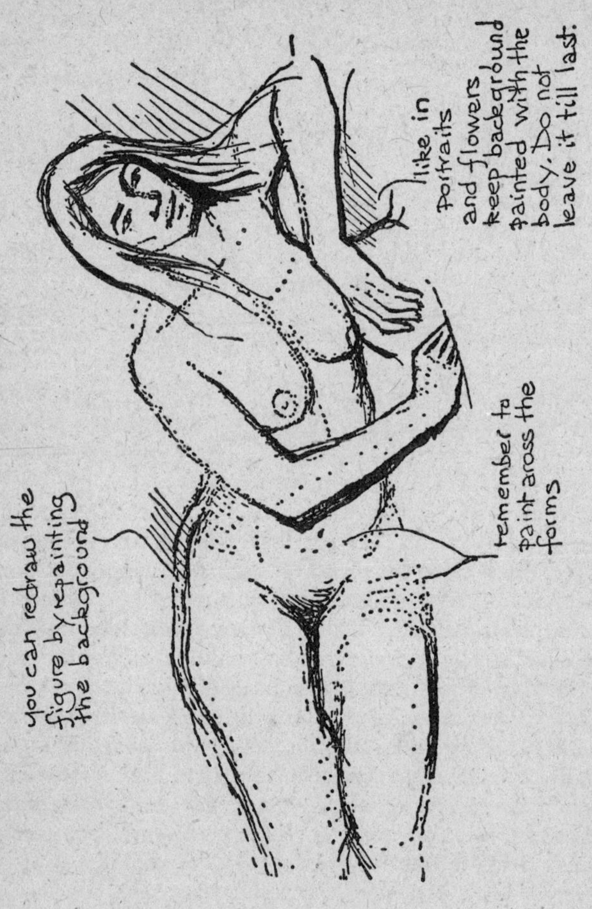

Fig. 64 Painting across the form.

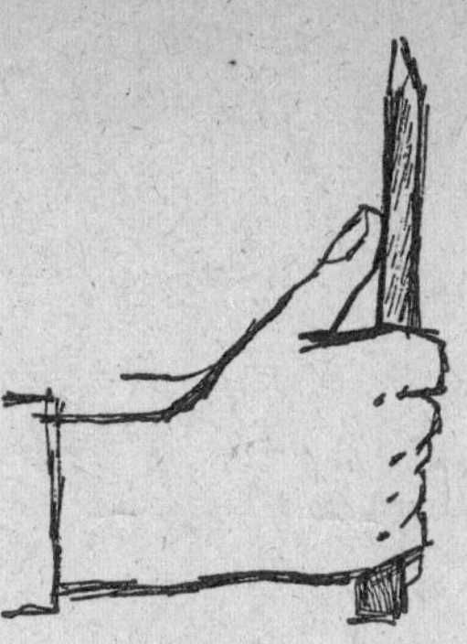

Fig. 65 In constructing an authentic composition *measure* relationships of man to machines, man to buildings, furniture, cars, etc.

advocated getting every relative proportion right. As in a portrait, it is possible to build up a whole figure by measurement (Fig. 63). Euan Uglow and Sir William Coldstream have painted nudes in this way.

While painting from the nude, draw with colour across the form (Fig. 64). Make experiments to give unusual colours by glazing thinly with warm flesh colours over cold underpainting; and *vice versa*.

Ingres wrote, 'The beautiful forms are those that have firmness and fullness; those in which the details do not compromise the aspect of the great masses.'

The bias of anyone writing about painting the nude usually appears to be towards the female nude. This, to an extent, is inherent in the European tradition. The female nude is an object of pleasure and the male nude heroic, especially in the great tradition of figure composition. Which leads to the next section.

THE FIGURE COMPOSITION

From about 1420 until the turn of this century the grand figure composition with elegantly disposed figure and inspiring subject matter, was considered the peak of any

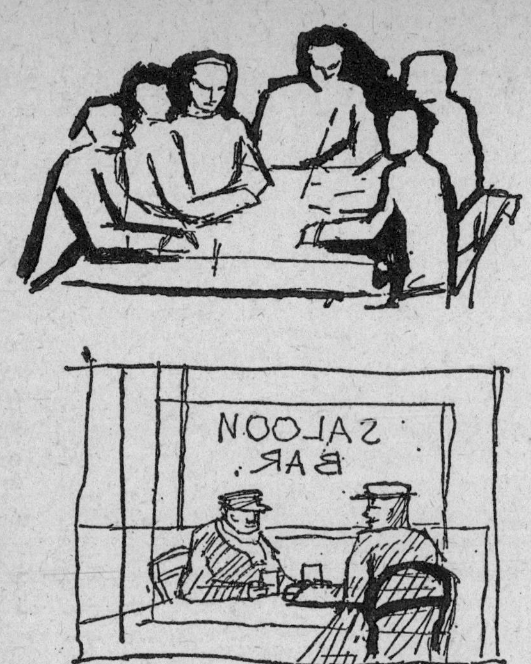

Fig. 66 Two sketches – one of boys in a study; another in a pub – how much space would *you* put round the figures to give convincing scale? The top one probably needs more space.

artist's achievement. However, the idea that a painting has, above all, to contain an ennobling idea is now not generally accepted. We now believe that a small still life can be as serious in content as a large figure painting. The great figure compositions of the past were contrived from drawings made directly from life. This is obvious, as it is quite impractical to have several models in a sort of *tableaux vivants*, posing for hour after hour. If you are painting a picture with figures you will probably have to rely on drawings (Fig. 65). The possible exception are the more informal domestic interiors. As this is within everyone's common experience it is worth some comment.

DOMESTIC SCENES, ETC.

For the moment we can base our plan of composition on the kind that fits shapes into the four edges of the board.

Lighting. Establish where the light is coming from, and keep the light constant, otherwise you will get into an awful muddle!

Scale. This is a question of how are you relating the figures to the interior (Fig. 66).

Bonnard's beautiful interiors are so well designed that he often ignores perspective and the picture still 'works'. If the perspective of interiors in the linear classical way is going to get you into difficulties, leave it. Rely instead on creating distance and depth by means of light (Fig. 67).

When you are composing figures in settings, you have to keep a balance between the figures and the surrounds. The advantage of a domestic interior is that you may be able to persuade friends or relations to pose for you. In painting domestic interiors, you could, like the contemporary artist Bernard Dunstan, paint small spontaneous pictures. In this way, you can capture the intimate character of everyday life. Vuillard and Sickert painted their enchanting interiors in this way, often using a coloured ground to effect middle tones.

Interiors do not of course have to be domestic but the more they are about places you cannot see constantly the more you must depend on drawings. This includes a wide range of human activity which are in our everyday experience, as well as subjects that are not. In the former, you could include factories, shops, cafés, etc. In the latter, are paintings of imagination and narrative – like Nativities or Last Suppers.

MORE ABOUT DRAWING FOR PAINTING

Carry a sketch book. This will mean you can take quick drawings of people working and playing; also animals as well as people. Draw as much as you can from life, the quick relevant poses of figures and hands that give character

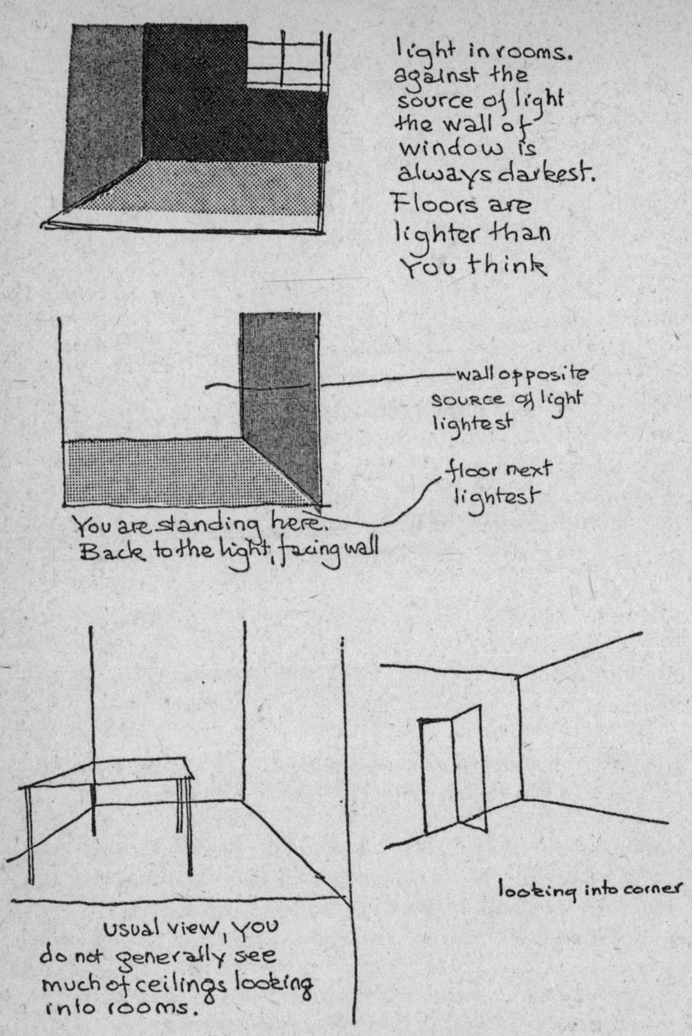

Fig. 67 Interior perspective.

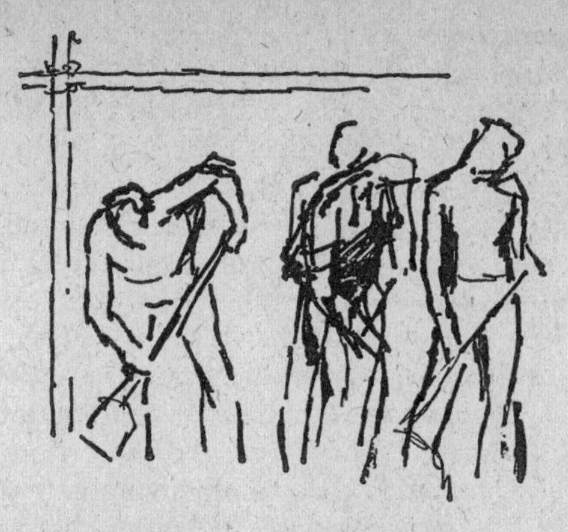

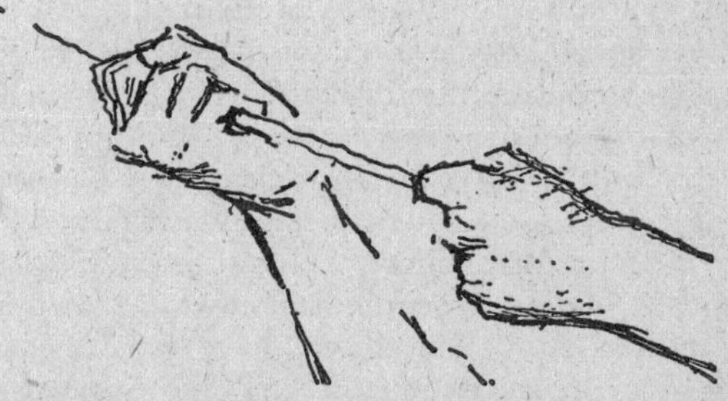

Fig. 68 In quick sketches of action, train your eye to see, and note down; size of tools, cars etc. in relation to figures.

to the subject (Fig. 68). Observe accurately comparative scale of people (or animals) in relation to interiors and objects; this gives authenticity to the painting.

You then have to work from these to make up a finished painting. One way is to do a complete drawing, and transfer it to your board. Sickert drew directly on to squared paper, which makes the problem of squaring up easier.

FIGURES IN LANDSCAPE

This subject calls to mind workers, farmers, animals,

bathers, picnickers. A subject with great possibilities. You have to be observant of relative scale. If you are painting figures out-of-doors you could treat this as a problem of the effect of light on figures, as one of the relationship of colour to light. There are two approaches. The first, obviously, of actually painting from the subject with the things in front of you, working very quickly. You would have to notice very accurately the relationship of colours, tones and shadows. The effect of light on flesh in sunlight is quite unexpected. Otherwise, you would have to reconstruct the effect of light. Seurat painted his great compositions in this way. He made many preliminary studies from nature. He most carefully noticed the complementary colours in shadows. Also the many variants of colour that one cloud contained. His paintings, in the finished result, are very brilliant expositions of the idea of light.

In any figure composition, inside or out, if you have quick sketch book studies of figures, it is very useful to get friends or a model to pose in those same positions again, to be able to take more accurate drawings. Unless you are painting on the spot, which is not always easy with many figures, the painting of figure composition entails contriving. This means finding an equivalent to direct painting, that works on the picture. That is, you have to paint a colour for flesh or grass or streets (or anything else) that works in the painting and looks right but may not be strictly true to natural appearance. A figure composition is still to a great extent a very good exercise. It imposes a discipline on one, and it is well worth trying at least once to carry such a composition through from start to finish. If you are working from drawings, at least you can keep the painting going over a stretch of time. If you have worked very hard at a life painting or composition, and you are disappointed with the result, never worry. No effort on any painting is lost; at all times one is learning something. Even unconsciously one is finding out about one's paint. Often enough the work put into a painting that seems to have gone entirely wrong, is repaid in the next painting. Earlier, the question arose of the spontaneous beginning that looks very good. As you go on painting, you will learn how often you can safely leave a brilliant beginning as it is – without, of course, letting this develop into the habit of never finishing anything!

PAINTING FROM PHOTOGRAPHS

By all means use photographs if they inspire you – but do take care not to copy the hard and shiny surface of the print too slavishly. Use photographs as guides for form and shape more than for surface texture. Photographs are, of course, very useful if you like painting things you do not see very often – wild animals, horses, sport, or the dance in various forms. Best of all, take your own photographs.

Photographs are often used by artists who like painting things that move very fast, i.e. racing cars, a football match or similar. The camera can capture movement. Chapter 5 gives you exercise in trying to make paint look as though it is moving. However, it is not entirely a good idea to only rely on the photograph. Whatever subject you take from a photograph, it should be backed up with something your own, like painting or drawn sketches from the subject. You can, of course, square up a photograph on to your board in exactly the same way as you can a drawing.

A COUPLE OF POINTS TO FINISH

There is nothing actually wrong with a smooth surface of oil paint. The way one actually uses one's paint is as intensely personal as one's handwriting. Every person responds to oil paint in their own way. Another reason why one should draw from a subject as well as using photographs, is that photographs distort scale. A drawing usually has a more authentic feeling for scale.

Painting figure compositions also includes other branches of painting, like landscape and townscapes. Of course, dividing up painting under subject heading is only for convenience, and the classifications should not be taken too literally.

The formal compositions in the grand style of the classic painters are still inspiring for their abstract qualities, i.e., line, rhythm, mass, tone, etc., though we probably do not wish to paint like them. The contemporary vision does not find much in common with concepts of the ennobling and the ideal. Generally we find more to inspire us in the come-and-go of everyday life. People at work, at play, with children, etc. These still, however, have to be composed, even informally. One can use a classic composition with a contemporary reference, as Manet did in his painting *Déjeuner sur l'herbe.*

A subject matter which can still take a formal treatment, is the heroic. In East European painting, one sees pictures that are of heroic subjects. It would seem that, by age-old tradition, paintings of war, death, heroism and work, demand a classic, elegaic treatment. It is likely that the rhythm of such paintings evokes solemn thoughts (Fig. 69). This sort of painting allows for a considerable amount of abstraction.

The whole assumption of this chapter has been that, despite fashion over the last thirty years, there is still as much to be painted from the human figure as at any time before.

The classic figure composition usually implies that the painting tells a story. Present century painters have, to a great extent, reacted against this. It was quite understandable that the first generation of modern painters – the Impressionists and post-Impressionists – should do so as the nineteenth century storytelling paintings, acceptable in the academies, were all too often completely lacking in artistic qualities.

There can, however, be no rule. If a story inspires you to paint then go ahead. Where illustrating alone can destroy artistic qualities is when you crowd a painting with details of the story, that distract from the totality of the whole. Whatever you paint bear in mind the basic rules. These are: tone, drawing (or *dessin* as it is in the French), form and

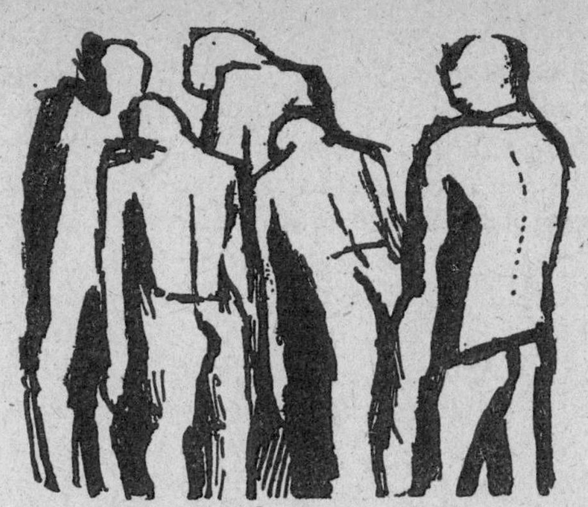

Fig. 69 'Heroic' composition.

colour. Even these could be ignored with enough intensity of vision (see next chapter).

One rule cannot be ignored: clean up your equipment! (It bears repeating!)

PAINTERS TO STUDY

Painters of the Nude and the grand formal composition:

Raphaël, Tintoretto, Titian, Velasquez, Veronese, Rubens, Delacroix

Painters of the Nude

Rembrandt, Courbet, Boucher, Manet, Ingres, Renoir, Gauguin

Painters of Interiors and Scenes from Everyday Life:

Among the very many Dutch interiors of the seventeenth century to be seen in museums, the especially great painters were Jan Vermeer, Pieter de Hooch.

Others include:

Velasquez, Frank Bramley, Chardin, Stanhope Forbes, Hogarth, W. R. Sickert, Vuillard, Bonnard, Matisse.

PAINTINGS TO LOOK AT

Nudes

Bristol Museum and Art Gallery: *Nude on Bed* by Spencer Gore.

Birmingham Art Gallery: *Study for Venus and Psyche* by Courbet.

Cambridge, Fitzwilliam Museum: *Venus and Cupid* by Palma Vecchio; *Venus and Cupid with Lute Player* by Titian.

Exeter, City Art Gallery: *Le Lit Cuivre* by Sickert.

London, National Gallery: *Origin of the Milky Way* by Tintoretto; *The Rokeby Venus* by Velasquez; *La Source* by Renoir.

London, Wallace Collection: *The Visit of Venus to Vulcan* by Boucher.

London, Courtauld Institute Gallery: *Nude* by Modigliani; *Reclining Nude* by Gauguin.

London, Tate Gallery: *Reclining Nude* by Victor Pasmore.

All museums in the British Isles have group paintings, Dutch interiors, and fine compositions. It is really impossible to choose. But if one had to, the following are truly outstanding examples: The Raphael Cartoons of the Acts of the Apostles, in The Victoria and Albert Museum, South Kensington, London, are the greatest works of high Renaissance Composition outside of Italy. Admittedly not oil paintings, but Raphael did work in oil paint. Then there are Poussin's *Seven Sacraments* in Edinburgh. A truly great Victorian painting in Manchester City Art Gallery, is Ford Maddox Brown's *Work*.

Perhaps the last painter of formal compositions of the figure is William Roberts, R.A. His work can be seen every year at the Royal Academy, London. Also, at the Royal Academy, look for the delightful interiors of Bernard Dunstan, R.A.

CHAPTER ELEVEN

ABSTRACTION AND MORE ABOUT USING PAINT

Some painters have very intense inner vision. This leads them to paint from imagination and fantasy: paintings that create a different world within the space of the picture. Usually they contain something of the external world, as means of decoding the painting. The things from the external world are either symbolic so that you read them like picture signs. Or they are actual but strangely distorted in some way. Painters who one thinks of as painters of fantasy are Bosch, John Martin and the later Goya (Blake of course was one but I am thinking only of oil painters) and some Grünewald. Each painted intense and entirely convincing paintings of hell or demons. To these painters the inner vision was more 'real' than the external world of 'facts'.

In the twentieth century the Surrealist painters are the painters of fantasy. They base their theories, rightly or wrongly, on the theories of Freud. Surrealist paintings generally are about imagery from the unconscious, the kind of strange things one may see in dreams when one has no control over one's thoughts. Some art historians see the visionary paintings of Bosch or Martin as the ancestors of surrealism. This is questionable. The paintings of Hell, however fantastic, expressed a belief that was common to everyone. The Surrealist vision expresses the private thoughts of the painter. If one has some driving urge to give one's private visions expression then one will do so. But it is disturbing when one visits contemporary galleries to see that this is what most modern paintings are about. There is no apparent wish to communicate to everyone in a common language of art. For all that, one must paint as one wants,

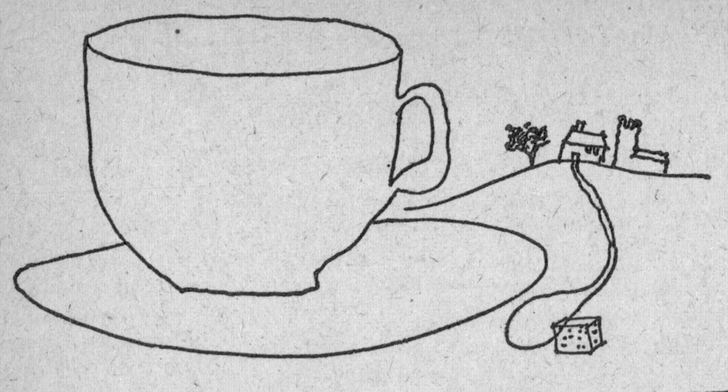

Fig. 70 To effect strangeness, scale is distorted. Familiar objects are put in unfamiliar contexts. Like a strange dream.

and so here are some comments on the painting of the fantastic, or the dream world. As I find this sort of painting exceedingly difficult, I hope the advice given will make it easier rather than otherwise.

Surrealist painters paint very smoothly, deliberately, one supposes, to imitate a photograph. By general consent, a camera cannot lie, so by this a painting that looks like a photograph must be true! Distortion is one of the basic characteristics of dream fantasy paintings (Fig. 70). Another method is the reading of the familiar in a different context. A Max Ernst painting in The Tate Gallery, London, has the texture of wood grain. Presumably the artist printed the texture from actual wood grain as one does with a lino-cut. Then a cerulean colour with white was painted behind the wood graining. By force of association and pre-knowledge, you read a forest, which is what the picture is titled. You can experiment with many textures in this way, printing them with oil paint (Fig. 71).

Other painters, like Klee and Miro, were interested in the ideas of the Surrealist painters. They tried to get back to

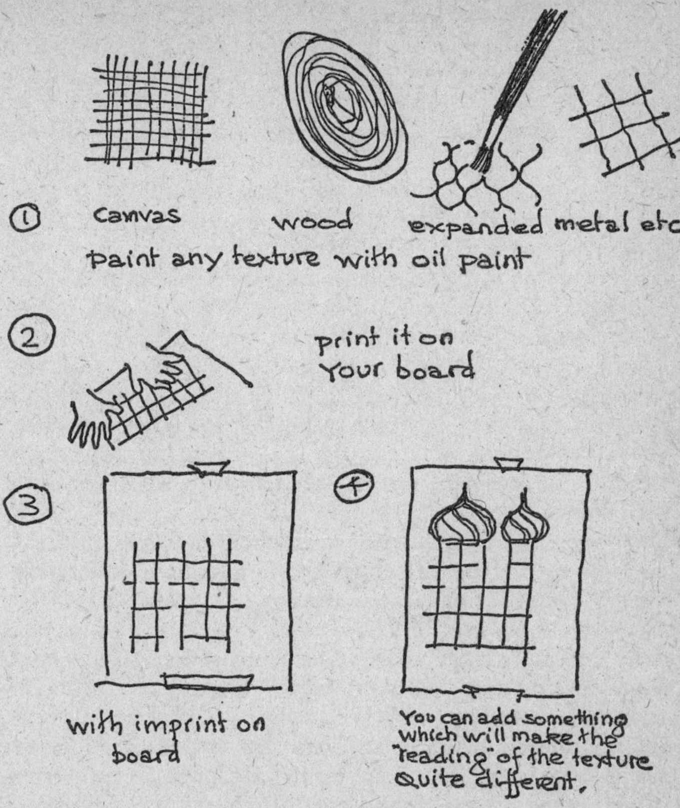

Fig. 71 Experimenting with textures.

more primal, even less conscious sources of art. Both were inspired by the art of children, and primitive artists. Of course, a child or a primitive artist paints in the way he does, unconsciously, or from unquestioned tradition; Klee and Miro's choice was entirely conscious. Their work has succeeded, because they were highly trained and skilful painters, who always knew, fantasy or otherwise, that in the end, you cannot disregard colour, tone, or design. Klee and

Miro's paintings are some of the most delightful examples of colour in twentieth century art. Both have humour, which you do not always find in very good painting.

Where a great number of visionary painters fail is that, in the end, they cannot attach their vision to the realities of board and paint. Surrealism then becomes just grotesque. There is rather the current belief that ugliness is more real than beauty. True or not, ugliness is certainly easier!

But to return to canvas and paint. A very fruitful offshoot of Surrealism is the American Abstract Expressionists. They were the first painters to paint purely from paint as first cause, rather than any reference to the external world. Some of the American painters, like Jackson Pollock, Rothko, De Kooning, have to be studied purely for what they did with the very nature of paint. Most of us somewhere have the primal urge to mess with paint, for its entirely tactile quality. This then is what the American Abstract Expressionists did for the first time in the history of oil painting (other media are not anything like as suitable).

Here then, if the idea appeals to you, are some suggestions to get you going with pure painting.

Start with an entirely blank board. With any colour you like, mix up a large amount on your palette. Take a large brush and fling the paint on. Choose another colour and do the same. Your very own personality will continue this sort of painting quite differently from somebody else. The idea is to go on painting till you get some sort of pattern of colour and tone (Fig. 72). Stand away from the painting, work round it. The painting may end up an awful mess. At any rate you will have learned that painting pure abstracts is not nearly as casual as it looks, or as easy. For making trailing dribbly lines that are very effective on a clear white or tinted ground, use tins of Valspar Enamel, which just about can come under the heading of 'oil painting'.

Sam Francis did the most beautiful paintings in entirely transparent glazes and stains of oil paint diluted in oil and turpentine. He never apparently mixed white with his oil paint at all. This is a way of getting the most delightful

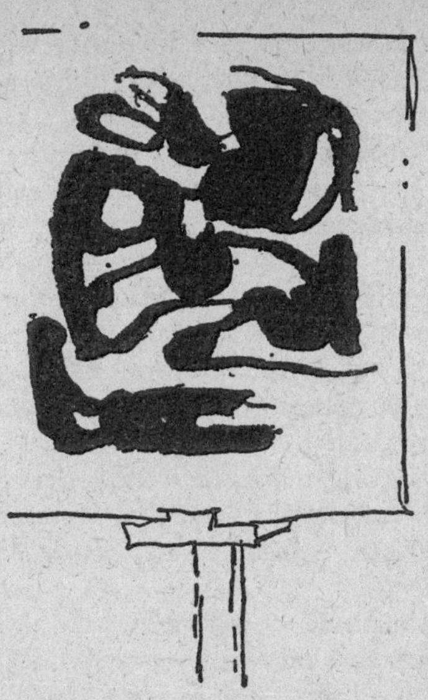

Fig. 72 Let the paint do what it wants. Let the paint tell you what to do next. Work from any angle and see which way painting looks best.

colours. If you have not discovered some unusual colours for yourself, here are some suggestions:

The first rule is, that you have to start with light colours, and build up darker. Obviously, the colours listed in Chapter Four as transparent are the most suitable.

For an unusual green: a yellow base, glaze with manganese blue.
A dark green: orange base, glaze with moastial blue.
A dark green: yellow base, glaze with indigo.
Blues: manganese base, glaze with violet.
Blues: violet base, glaze with indigo.
Reds: yellow base, glaze with rose or crimson.
Reds: orange base, glaze with magenta.
Neutral darks: Indigo base, glaze with raw umber.
Neutral darks: Winsor green base, glaze with violet.

And of course, the many others you can find for yourself. These colours can be mixed, but the result is not quite the same.

At the other extreme, here are some suggestions if you like getting carried away by very thick paint, and really becoming involved with the texture. Painting very thickly is not a recommendation for permanence, so be warned. Many painters who use paint thickly, like to paint on in slabs with palette knives or painting knives. Fun to do, but after a time the paint will change, and is even inclined to wrinkle. If you are quite indifferent to durability, you can mix paint to a cement-like paste with Polyfilla, or a like product. In this case it is pointless using high quality artist colours. Tins of coarse-ground oil paint for scene painting are perfectly suitable.

For a reasonably durable texture to the paint, you can add either pumice powder or sand. Both give a gritty surface that is more effective in painting on a large scale.

Polyfilla, sand and pumice powder are ruinous to paint brushes. Either use very cheap or very old brushes that do not matter, or a palette knife.

Many of you may want to experiment with textures, paint etc., but feel that this is difficult without some definite idea how to start. This therefore leads on to another aspect of abstract painting.

ABSTRACT AND FIGURATIVE

Much of the painting that we call abstraction is in fact based on things in the external world. There are many things in the world of which we have an almost primal pre-knowledge or idea, without even going to look at them. This is how children paint. Such subjects include houses, chairs, bottles, fruit, people, birds, boats, trees and flowers. These objects are clear and well defined, mostly man-made and traditional. You can probably think of more to add to the list. These things then, can be used in paintings in a great number of variations without losing their recognisable qualities. This then is the basis of much abstract painting, especially among the German Expressionists, and many French painters of the early twentieth century.

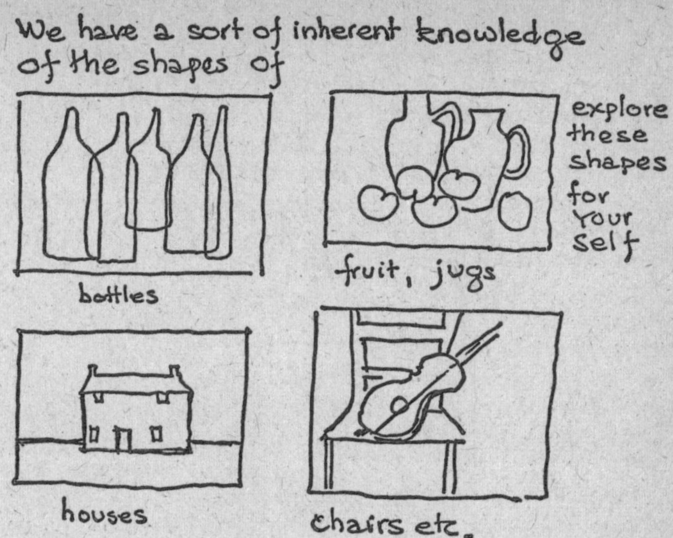

Fig. 73 Exploring shapes.

The basic idea is quite simple; that you start out with a motive and then experiment (Fig. 73). Of course, it is not easy to produce a good painting, but the experiment is very well worth while. You come back to the problem posed in the previous chapter of composing a painting shape for shape.

This sort of painting is mostly flat, and is not concerned with extension and depth. So, if you like the idea of painting towns, or boats where a literal painting would involve perspective which you may find formidable, here is a solution to one part of the problem (Fig. 74).

Tone, as you have seen, is frequently used to give depth and solidity. However, even if you are painting an entirely flat painting with no suggestion of depth, tones of colours are still essential (Fig. 75). This is what gives Matisse's and Braques' paintings quality and life even in black and white photographic reproduction.

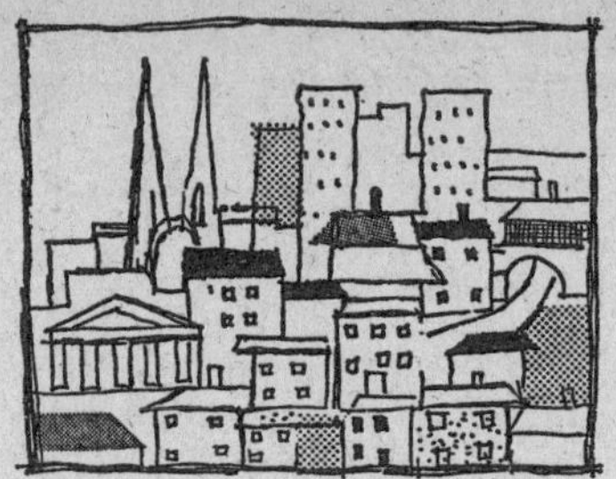

Fig. 74 Use tone, textures, colours, line.

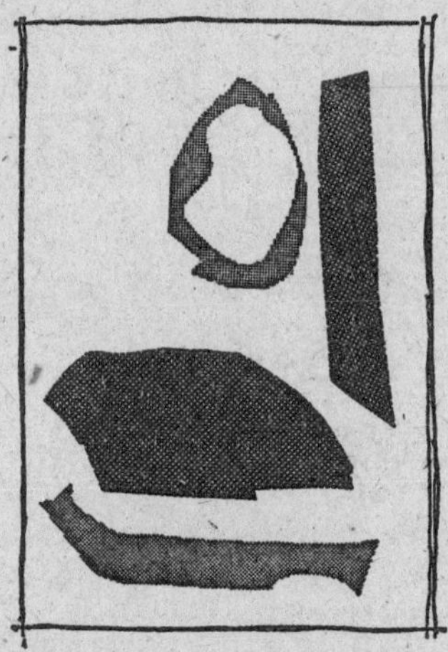

Fig. 75 Abstract, figurative – textured, transparent. You must look for tonality of colour! Tone influences shape.

In this sort of abstract painting the line between it and figurative painting is narrow. Many painters start by drawing from nature the things they will eventually abstract. This is quite usual. In the same way a painting started directly from nature can be reduced to its abstract forms in the studio, away from the subject. Braque painted many, many paintings of conceptual images. His still lifes always delight through their vigorous shapes and in some cases Braque uses conceptual colours, like the very obvious ones

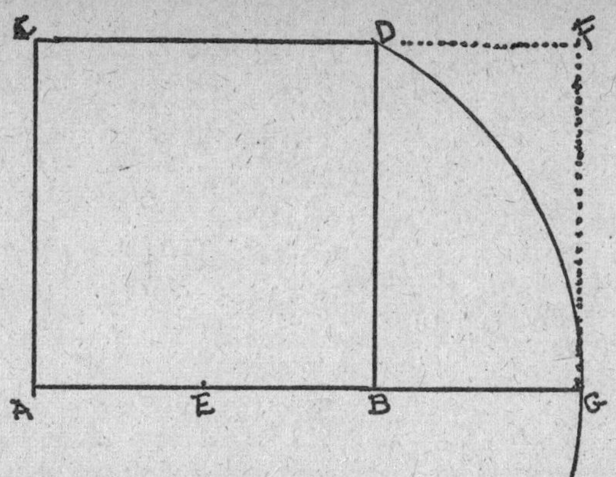

Fig. 76 The Golden Section.

of lemons and apples. In others, by retaining a recognisable shape, he changes colours to suit the picture. The last point is worth repeating. One can take things a long way to make a picture look 'right'. To remind you, Braque also used texture in his paintings to vary the surface.

Many painters whose work is quite non-figurative, have started out painting more or less from nature. Among these are the Dutch painter Mondrian and his closest follower, Ben Nicholson. At first sight their paintings appear entirely remote from figurative painting, but, in fact, they have a lot in common with the works of man. Among man's basic building forms are the horizontal and vertical. Nicholson's paintings are concerned with one of the traditions of European art, proportion. It is possible to paint a picture by dividing the board into its proportional parts, to make

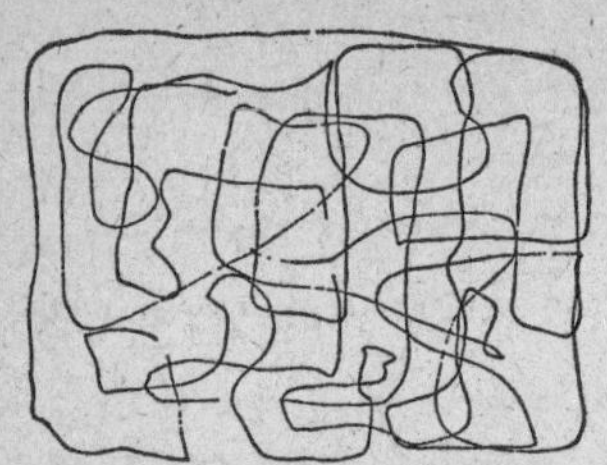

Fig. 77 A new way of drawing using line as line on your picture surface. Not to draw anything in particular.

the end result as agreeable as possible. A form of proportion that the classical architects found satisfying was the Golden Section (Fig. 76). However it is used, it looks 'right'.

Once having divided your board, you could go on by experimenting with harmonious colours, and balancing colour and tone.

Mondrian wrote a great deal. In one essay he compares his vertical and horizontal paintings to landscape. When one thinks of his native Holland, this is quite a reasonable claim. In another essay, more understandably, he compares his paintings to a great metropolis. A great city does indeed make one think of horizontals and verticals. To come back to your painting or mine for that matter. Try doing a painting of horizontals and verticals. So easy in one's mind, and yet when I actually tried, after an hour or so the amateurish result was shaming indeed.

To develop this from Chapter 5. You could make a painting in variations of one colour.

Or contrasting colours. Make an experiment with the boundaries of colours on your board.

Comparative densities of colours. Start with a board entirely painted in one colour. Stand back and look at the colour. You could add an area of a neutral. Or a similar colour. Another idea is to draw with your paint brush a wandering line however it takes you (Fig. 77).

With all these experiments you could still use images from the external world, reduced to their simplest elements.

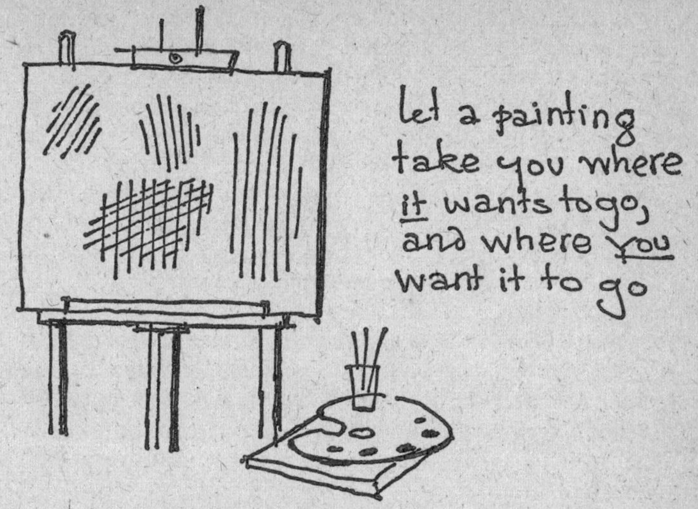

Fig. 78 Let a painting take you where it will.

Perhaps the painting will change completely. Perhaps it will turn into something else. In some kinds of painting, and some pictures you have to let the painting take you where it will (Fig. 78).

Conceptual images from the external world can be used for paintings of fantasy. A painter who comes to mind in this context is Chagall. His fantasies are far from private. On the contrary, he must be the only painter in history whose imagery has given a name to a highly successful musical comedy, *Fiddler on the Roof*. Chagall's images, clear and direct, belong to a whole people. So it is still possible today to paint images in a common idiom. It is a vision so intensely personal that no book on how to paint can tell you. However, a book cannot tell you often enough, that your vision MUST also be in terms of canvas and paint, colour, tonality and composition.

Perhaps, one should end this chapter with a word or two on Pop Art, though an element of doubt lies in the fact that much of Pop Art has not been painted in oil paint. Most of the pop paintings are in acrylics, and other media. Pop Art is another of the names of art movements of the twentieth century. It originated in America. Through an interchange of artists from Britain to America, maybe due to a spoken language in common, the movement became Anglo-American. The imagery of Pop is taken from advertising, comic strips and the lowest level of various media. Whether the Pop artists are really trying to create an art for the ordinary folk, you, me and everyone else, is difficult to say. Supposing you do find that Pop Art is for you, then here are a few suggestions: always use clear, bright colours, and make a point of collecting photographs, and advertisements. It may be, of course, that by the time this book is published Pop Art could be out of date!

PAINTERS TO LOOK AT (Oil paintings only)

PAINTERS OF FANTASY

Bosch. 1450–1516. Flemish School.
H. Fuseli. 1741–1825. British School.
Goya. 1746–1828. Spanish School.
J. Martin. 1789–1854. British School.
O. Redon. 1840–1916. French School.

SURREALIST PAINTERS

S. Dali. b. 1904. Spanish School.
M. Chagall. b. 1887. Russian-French School.
Max Ernst. b. 1881.
Paul Nash. 1889–1946. British School.
G. Sutherland. b. 1903. British School.
Stanley Spencer. b. 1881–1959. British School.

ABSTRACT EXPRESSIONISM

Jackson Pollock. 1912–1956.
M. Rothko. 1903–1970.
A. Gorky. 1904–1948.

ABSTRACT FROM NATURE

Picasso. b. 1882.
Braque. 1882–1963.

OTHER ABSTRACT PAINTERS

P. Mondrian. 1872–1944. Dutch School.

Ben Nicholson. b. 1898. British School.

All the above painters are represented in London, either in the Tate Gallery, or the National Gallery. Paintings outside London that are well worth seeing are listed below. Stanley Spencer's work can be seen in many galleries, as can that of Paul Nash, Graham Sutherland and Ben Nicholson.

Birmingham Museum and Art Gallery: *Le Lecture* by Marcoussis.

Bristol City Art Gallery: *Newlyn Harbour* by Bryan Wynter.

Cardiff, Nat. Gal. of Wales: *Flower Decoration* by Duncan Grant.

Glasgow, Art Gallery: *Still Life with Apples* by Braque.

Edinburgh, Museum of Modern Art: *Untitled* by Robert Motherwell.

Newcastle, Laing Art Gallery: *The Bard* by John Martin.

CHAPTER TWELVE

SEASCAPES AND TOWNSCAPES

All great art tells us more about ourselves. Turner's lifelong obsession with the sea in all its moods, tells us how primal water is to man. Looking at any Turner painting, it is clear that his vision has almost become one with his paint. There appear to be no rules and every rule: but one is clear: relentless observation.

The sea, particularly, is an aspect of nature where we can find the moods of man most reflected. Calm, sparkling gaiety, fury, etc. Van Gogh wrote in a sermon when he was a priest 'Our early life is like sailing on a river; but very soon

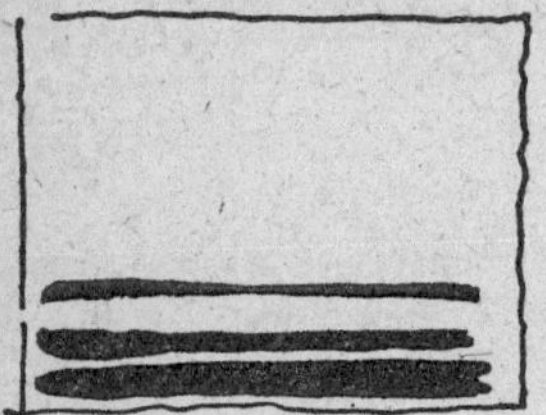

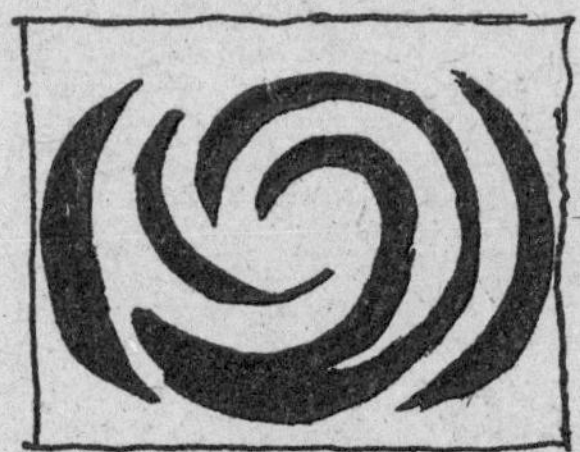

Fig. 79 The two basic forms of sea. Horizontal calm (*left*) and Movement (*right*).

the waves become higher, the wind more violent, we are at sea before we are aware of it. God, my bark is so small and Thy sea is so great. The heart of man is much like the sea, it has its storms, its tides, its depths; it has its pearls too.'

Vision, mood and poetic feeling must of course, be expressed in paint and board. As with other aspects of painting where how one sees the subject is so dependent on light, the following approaches are suggested. Work from several small sketches to make one big painting. If there is a

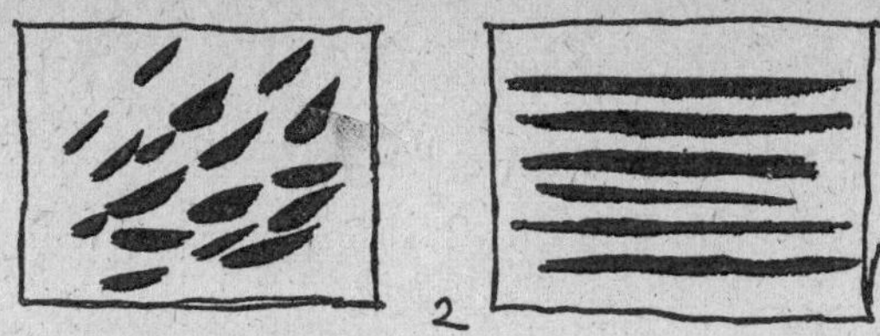

Fig. 80 (1) Brush strokes for movement.
(2) Brush strokes for calm.
(3) White lead is very good for getting involved with painting thick textured paint for waves and foam.

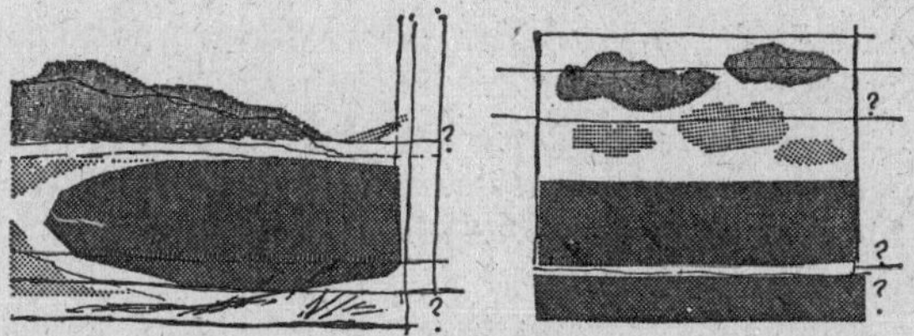

Fig. 81 How would you go about composing these? Where would *you* cut the picture?

disadvantage to this method, it may be loss of spontaneity. Also, when one paints from nature directly, one is more likely to paint what one sees. On coming away from the subject, this is the very first thing that one is apt to paint out, as some contrary instinct persuades one that it could not be real. But then, as mentioned before, many painters, including Bonnard (who, incidentally, painted many very beautiful seascapes) found nature so confusing that after a time they were obliged to paint away from the subject. Once more, therefore, one comes back to the authenticity of an artist's vision.

Painting the sea directly, the following observations may give direction to your painting:

A cloudy day makes for shadows across the sea.

Look out for unexpected changes of tone in the water, especially at the horizon.

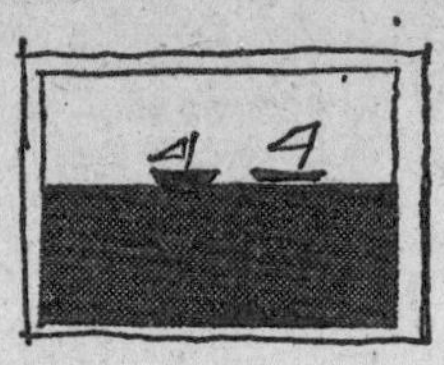

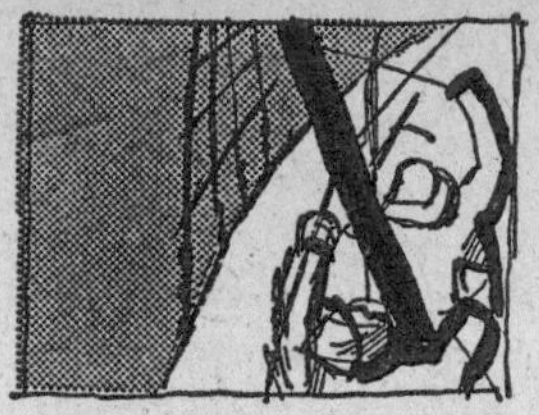

Man and his works give scale to seascapes.

Fig. 82 Man and his works give scale to seascapes.

Sun on the sea, by contrast, brings out the most beautiful complementary colours. This can depend on the nature of the water too. Some places like Cornwall and the Mediterranean have particularly clear water, which reflects to a particularly intense blue. A southern sea has fewer changes of mood.

At sunset you sometimes find the unusual effect of the sea being lighter than the sky.

Turner created the most convincing effects of sea by the very way he handled the paint. Paint is thrown on in a way that almost imitates the effect of waves and foam.

Glazing can be used to delightful effect to give the transparency of water. Brush marks can evoke movement or calm (Fig. 80).

At risk of being repetitive one comes back to the question of tone and composition. The most subtle and observant seascapes have been based on very simple compositions and tones.

It is an instructive exercise to compose a seascape as the parts are deceptively simple (Fig. 81).

Turner gave scale to his paintings by the addition of figures. Turner was a true romantic, where man was dwarfed by the vastness of nature. Fear was mixed with an almost religious awe. Figures and boats are painted deliberately small in relation to the picture space. Man and his works give scale to any sea or landscape (Fig. 82).

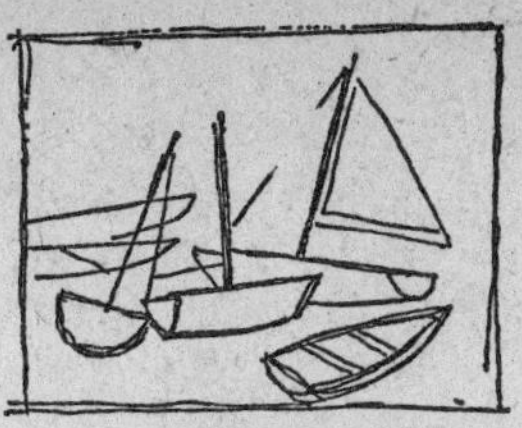

Fig. 83 Boats can take schematising and abstracting without losing their recognisability.

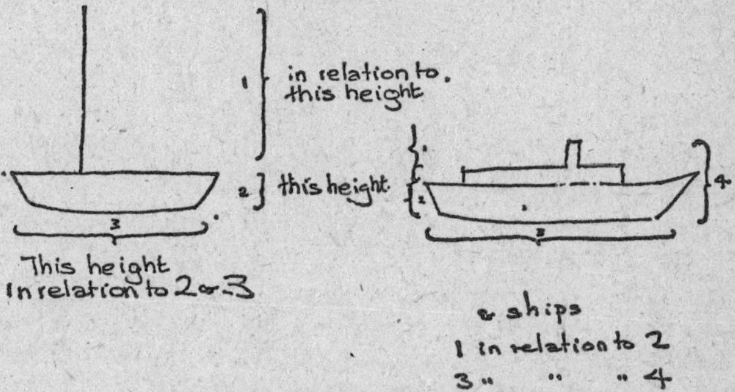

Fig. 84 This is how to measure boats. A useful rule of thumb.

To many artists, boats are as much an inspiration to paint as the sea itself. Indeed, one of the first paintings that made me interested in painting was Van Gogh's painting of gay little fishing boats. To judge by the number of prints that sell of boats of all kinds, they are a source of pleasure and response to many, many people. Boats are as much basic works of man as a house or water pot, and it is right that we respond to them.

Boats, like some of the other things mentioned in the last chapter, can take a lot of varying without losing their identity (Fig. 83). This should be a consoling thought to anyone who finds perspective difficult. However, to other painters the intricacy of boats and ships is the very thing that makes them inspiring. In this case you will need perspective. Equally important is proportion.

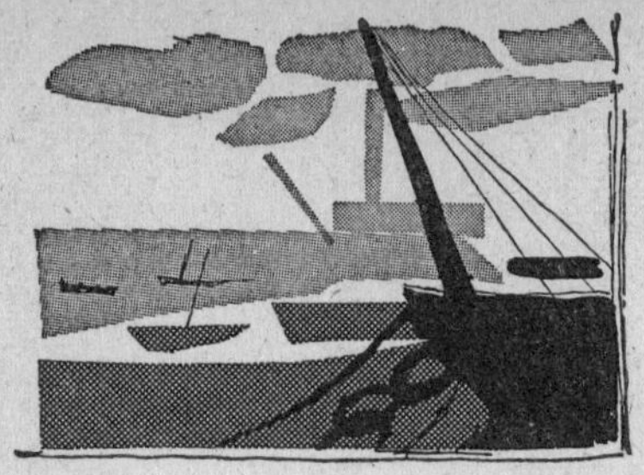

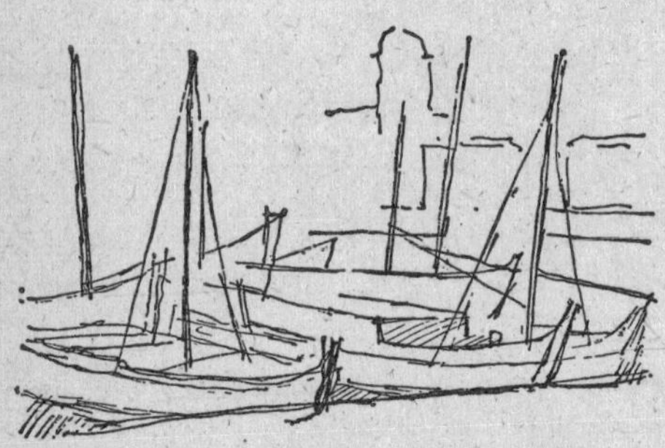

Fig. 85 Composition for boats and ships.

Measure length against breadth; masts against length. Remember that what may be accurately measured may not always look 'right' in the painting (Fig. 84). An example of this odd fact is drawing a line exactly down the middle of the board. It may well not look half and half. Boats and ships of all kinds present the most intriguing problems of composition (Fig. 85).

You will see that the subject has many, many variations. In every museum in the country you can see fine old pictures, often by Dutch artists, of sailing ships. When they were painted, sailing ships were the norm. In Holland, the prosperity of the whole country was through trade. Ships (like, indeed, paintings of tulips!) were then part of the

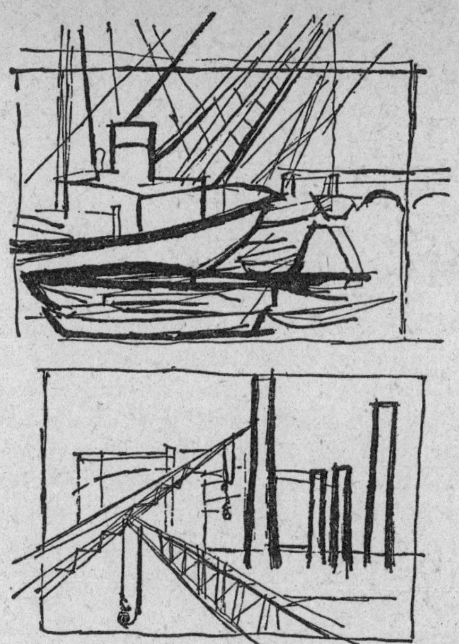

Fig. 86 Two sketches. One of a dockyard; the other of factories. Both these could be taken further. Either more figuratively; or more abstract. Depending on your inclination.

economics of everyday life. Some painters today are rightly fascinated by these magnificent old ships. The difficulty is reconstructing a painting with any real degree of authenticity. If you want to paint old ships, you should make every effort to consult contemporary books and prints of ships, as well as paintings.

Museums also have the most delightful primitive paintings of boats. They were painted by all kinds of folk; sailors themselves, signwriters and others. One can be inspired by their clarity and vitality. But, of course, no one can suddenly decide to 'be' a primitive – it is something you either are or are not. Attempts to go primitive are in most cases failures.

Great modern ships and docks are inexhaustible subjects

for paintings. Cranes, funnels, vistas of sky and industry are always inspiring. This is the kind of seascape where the ships and buildings give the scale rather than the other way about. If you are painting from nature directly you are dependent on effects of light. A rule of thumb that is useful in any painting outside is to divide the light according to time of day: early morning, mid morning, afternoon, and evening. Where light changes, colour changes. While you are painting in a changing light, you should settle for a time in the course of your painting where you do not alter sea or sky drastically any more. Once the painting is on its way, settle for a more or less stable cloud and sea formation and tone and colour. If you keep altering, the difficulty is that you may end up with nothing conclusive. Another thing you can find, is that if you paint for too long, you may suddenly find that the light has altered and everything looks quite different. It is as well then, if you are out painting for a whole day, to paint a couple of paintings – one for morning and the other for evening or sunset. In very grey days this does not apply.

Ships, factories, docks, are subjects that also lend themselves to semi-abstraction (Fig. 86) depending on the way you paint.

These subjects are also, of course, related to townscapes, which form the second part of this chapter.

TOWNSCAPES

Many thousands of paintings of Paris are sold every year to tourists. Their appeal is not that they are always works of great merit. It is usually that the painter has conveyed the flavour and atmosphere of the city. This is much easier written than described, let alone taught in a book. However, I will try. Affection for the place you are painting is an obvious ingredient.

CHARACTER OF TOWNS

The character of a town is not necessarily in its finest

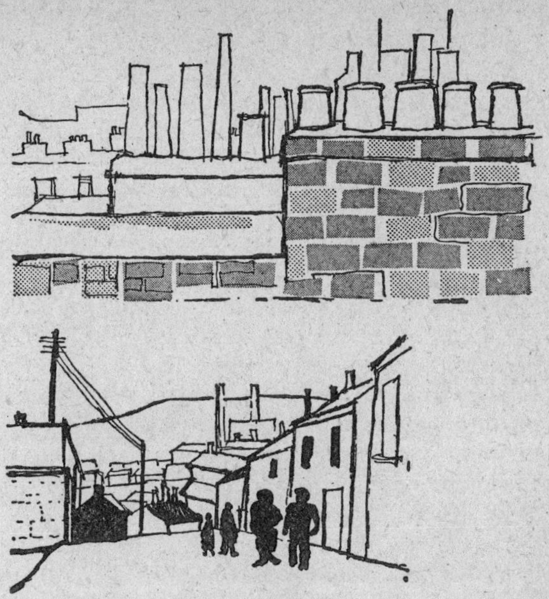

Fig. 87 Something personal that *you* associate with a place. Chimney pots or wide streets, etc.

buildings. You may associate something particular with a place, chimney stacks, wide streets, etc.

Some cities have their own colour – or rather a colour one always associates with them. Painters who have noticed this in London were Monet and Whistler. They were both fascinated by the effects of fog. This was also true of Turner. To Monet's eye, the effects of mist and fog were analysed in terms of the Impressionist theories of colour. Whistler painted the muted effects of the blues, browns, and greys of fog. He noticed that a fog or mist narrows tonal range. Whistler's pupil and disciple was W. R. Sickert, who painted with obvious affection the shabby back streets of Camden Town and Islington. Where you are painting does

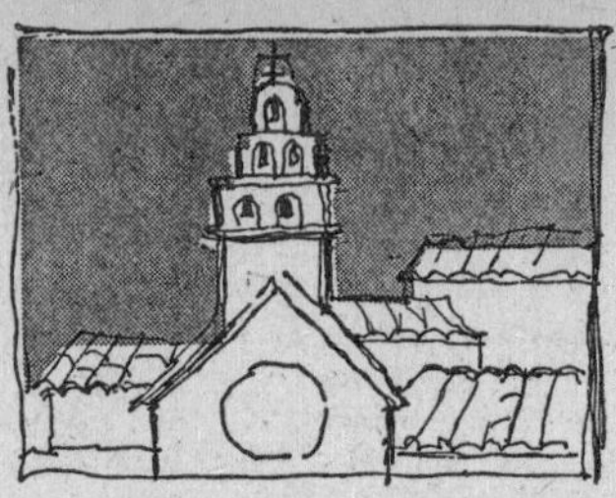

Fig. 88 In the south, the blue sky is often darker than the buildings and the country.

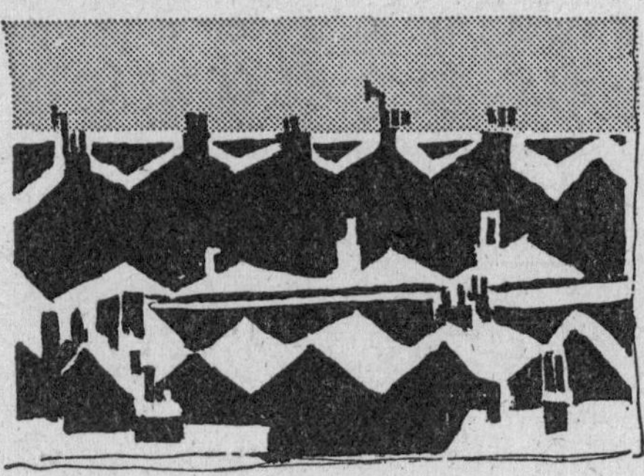

Fig. 89 Snow makes delightful patterns in cities. The snow is the lightest thing in the picture. Equate it to the white on your palette.

not of course need to be a famous capital city; it can be anywhere. The important thing is observation – look for colour, light, and the very thing you believe to be characteristic of the place you are painting (Fig. 87).

While generally ignoring the conventional rules of perspective and proportion, Lowry, the northern painter, has such an intense feeling for industrial landscape that he has made us see things we would not have seen without his vision.

The following colours and their mixture are always useful in painting buildings:

Raw umber, yellow ochre, light red, permanent sepia. Flesh colour – which is a pale terra cotta – is useful too.

These earth colours are very similar to the colours of buildings, on their own or mixed with white.

LIGHT IN CITIES

In some cases this is the same as colour. In the south or on very sunny days, the sky is darker in tone than the buildings, so you get a darker tone at the top of the picture space (Fig. 88). In the south too, you find the buildings very sharply contrasted with shadows. You will probably find that the buildings throw very blue shadows contrasted to the warmth of the light.

Usually, in northern towns – the buildings are darker than the sky. One often finds roofs, chimney pots and television aerials falling into delightful compositions.

Snow is as delightful to paint in town as in the country. It is madc casy by the fact that you have the absolute white that you equate to the white on your palette (Fig. 89). All other tones are graded accordingly. The sky, in this case is darker than the snow.

Of the Continental painters who noticed the colours of individual cities, Utrillo painted the greys of Paris. He painted Paris at a time when many painters and writers congregated there, and one could live very cheaply. One only has to look at a good painting by Utrillo (there are countless bad ones or forgeries, a wry tribute to his popularity) to be reminded of the world of Hemingway, Henry Miller, Elliot Paul. A good Utrillo painting is worth studying for the many ways in which he handled paint. Here are some of them (Fig. 90):

Paint is put on with a palette knife to remind you of crumbling stucco.

Stippled paint makes an unusual texture but be warned against using it too much, as the effect can become overpowering.

White is painted thinly over warm colours to get greys.

Bonnard and Vuillard painted unusual views of streets and little squares, with ordinary folk about their everyday

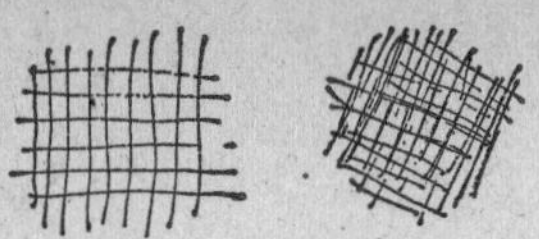

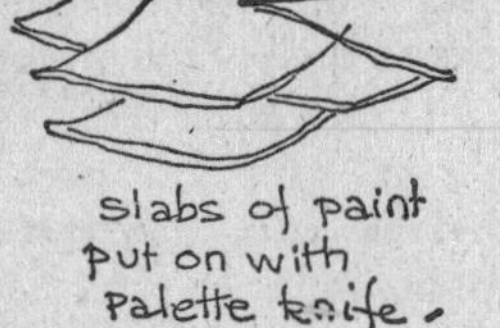

Fig. 90 Textures in oil paint.

lives. I would like to stress this point, as it is very easy to look at French paintings, and think there must have been something special about Paris. There was to its natives, as it was their home. Anywhere can be special if it means something to *you*. The most depressing paintings of towns are the ones where the painter has tried to pretend it was Paris, and has not really looked any deeper.

ARCHITECTURAL PAINTING

Among the greatest painters of the eighteenth century were Canaletto, Guardi, and Bellotto. All were Venetians, though Canaletto worked in England and Bellotto in Warsaw. When Warsaw was rebuilt after 1945, it was reconstructed almost entirely from Bellotto's paintings: a lasting tribute to a painter's accuracy and skill. These three Venetian painters are as popular now, either in print or in the originals (for those who can afford them), as they were when their works were painted. Here a historical difficulty arises. We look at them now as a reminder of a time when London or Venice were particularly elegant (though smelly!). Of course, the painters were painting their subjects as they saw them. Today, if we paint a large and imposing

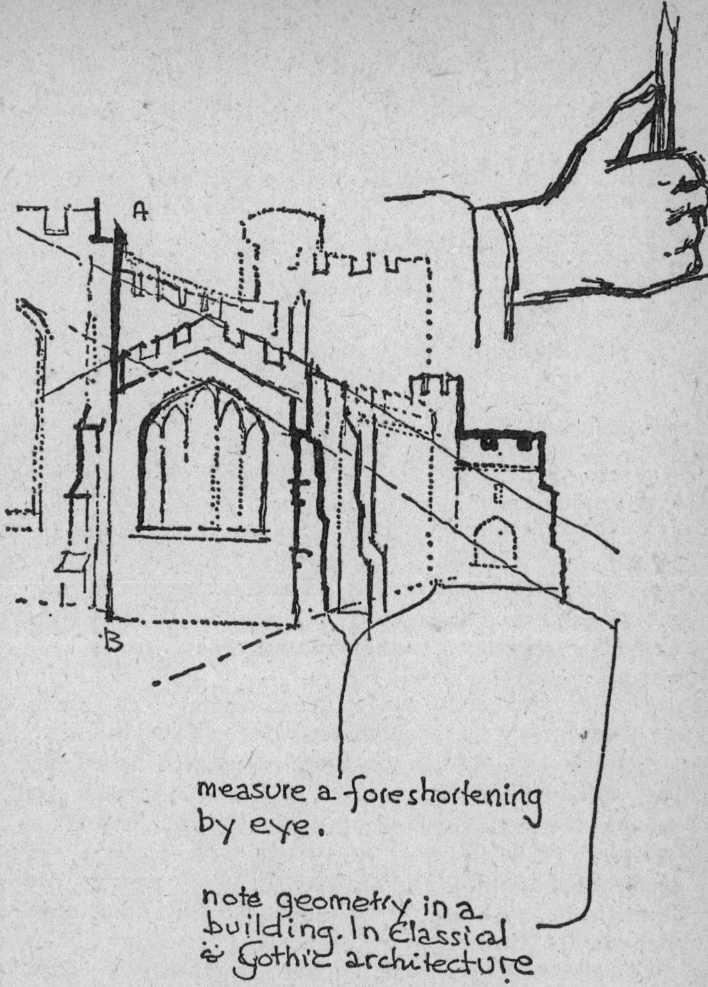

Fig. 91 Rules of thumb for measuring buildings.
Take any one vertical, e.g. line A.B to measure the other verticals by.
Take all other measurements in relation to this one.
Width of windows in relation to height.
Greatest height of whole building against greatest width.

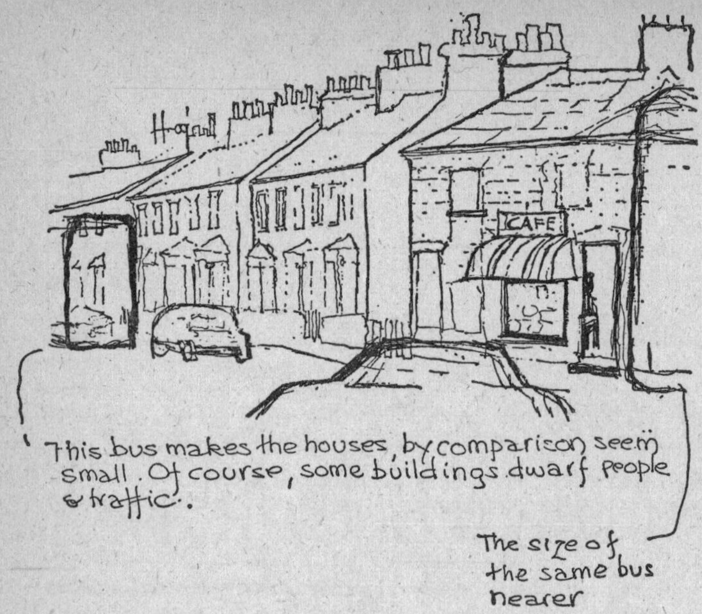

Fig. 92. Comparative proportion.

picture of exact architectural detail, we have to include tower blocks and traffic of all kinds. Not to do so, would be to paint an elaborate forgery ignoring the present. For all that, let's begin painting. . . ,

If you are painting a townscape with a fine vista of a cathedral or the Houses of Parliament or the like, you cannot avoid the problem of perspective. If you enjoy the problems of perspective as many painters do, so much the better.

Proportion is an absolute essential. For individual buildings (see Fig. 91).

Also important is comparative proportion, e.g. tower blocks in relation to shorter buildings, motor cars and buses in relation to width of streets (Fig. 92).

Composition. Decide if a particular building is going to

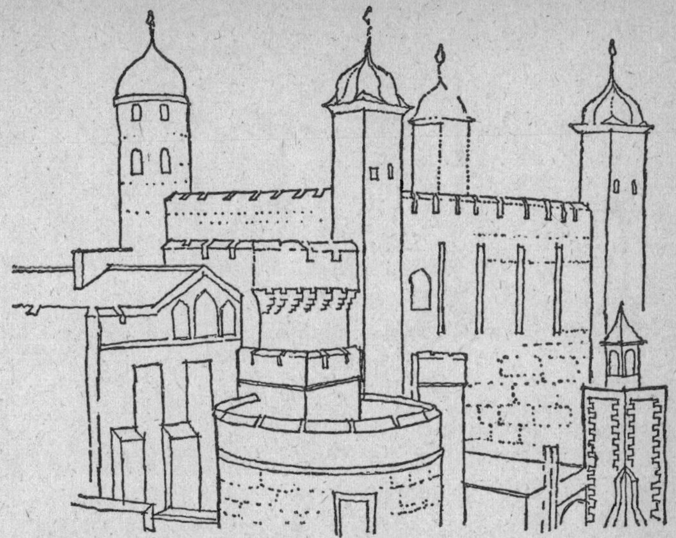

Fig. 93 There are times when you must make careful working drawings for architectural paintings. This one is from the Tower of London.

dominate the whole painting. This may easily happen in a cathedral city. Decide how much town you show in relation to sky.

Painting. If you are painting an elaborate architectural study, decide if you will be able to keep going back to the subject itself to finish the painting. You probably could in a city where the weather was stable. Otherwise make plenty of working drawings (Fig. 93).

It might be sensible to draw out on your board the whole painting first in line. An architectural painting, of course, depends greatly on the drawn line. You should see that the line is flexible and varied. An even, mechanical line is deadening and depressing (Fig. 94).

As in any other landscape settle for a particular light. Use the shadows cast by buildings as part of the tonal composition (Fig. 95).

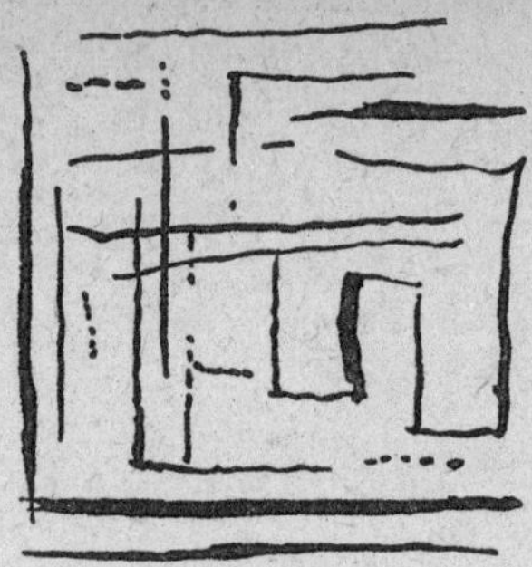

Fig. 94 Lines drawn with a sable brush. Sable is particularly good for drawing springy vital lines.

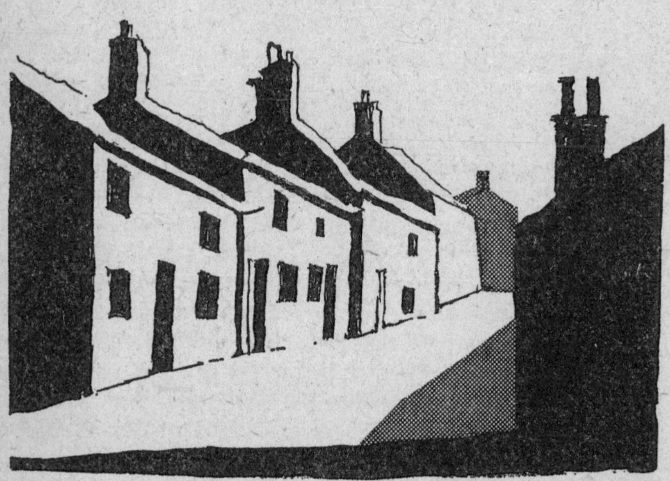

Fig. 95 You can compose townscapes with shadows cast by buildings, and the patterns they make. Look out for colour in shadows too!

There is another approach to painting in cities. Anyone who has seen the Expressionist painter Kokoschka's paintings of London river, and Hamburg will see that you can take yet another approach to painting cities, or indeed anything

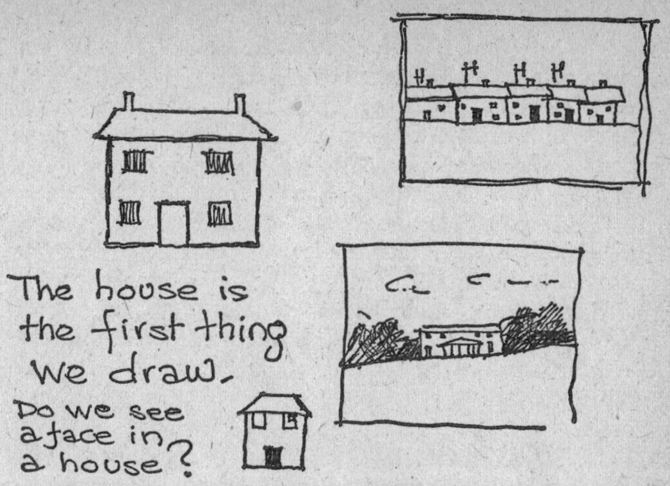

Fig. 96 Houses.

else. It would appear that Kokoschka has no theories like the Impressionist Monet. He paints, as it were, his own feelings that have come through the thing seen and the paint. Something in what the painter has seen with as much his feeling eye as his seeing eye, have inspired the painting. A smear of paint or a large stroke with a paint-filled brush has somehow made us read sky or smoking chimney stacks. Like many Expressionist painters, Kokoschka does not always paint the colours of nature – as they are. If it suits his feeling, he changes the colours. If looking at something for an entirely private reason makes you want to paint it a different colour, do so – providing it is 'right' within the terms of the painting. Constable once observed 'Every original picture is a separate study, and is governed by laws of its own. What is right in one, would be entirely wrong if transferred to another.' Though Constable actually said this about a landscape it could be said about any other painting.

As well as the city, it is worth mentioning the house. A

dwelling house is a basic expression of man's life on earth. It can be any house: grand, old or modern. It can be the houses around one, with gardens and flowers. Or cottages or streets with terraced houses. There is something basic in a house, as in a child's drawing (Fig. 96). If you are inspired (or, as likely, commissioned) to paint a grand house in its own grounds; you have the problem of combining landscape with building. Landscape in this case should take precedence. The house will give the landscape scale.

Much underestimated subjects in painting are aeroplanes of all descriptions. Their shapes and clarity of colours lend themselves to a high degree of abstraction, and would also be a delight to anyone who enjoys *really accurate* technical drawing.

PAINTERS TO LOOK FOR

Seascape and townscape painters worth looking at are very well represented in this country. As this book is about oil painting, remember that fine water colour studies of architecture cannot be properly included.

Birmingham, Museum and Art Gallery: *St. Jacques, Dieppe* by Sickert; *St. Maria della Saluta i Dogana* by Guardi; *Sunset Over Bridge* by C. Pisarro; *Industrial Townscape* by L. S. Lowry.

Bristol, City Art Gallery: *L'Eternité* by Courbet.

Cardiff, National Museum of Wales: *Twilight* by Monet; *Sunset Over Cathedral* by Monet.

Glasgow Art Gallery: *Village Street* by Utrillo.

Hull Museum: *Entrance to River Hull* by John Ward (the marine painter).

Hull, Ferens Gallery: A large collection of many fine marine paintings.

Liverpool : if you are in that area, or Manchester, look out for the paintings of Atkinson Grimshaw, who has an amazing sense of the flavour of Liverpool.

Leeds, City Art Gallery: *The Port of Marseilles* by Marquet; *Storm Over Scheveningen* by van Ruysdael.

Manchester City, Art Gallery: *An Island* by L. S. Lowry.
Newcastle, Laing Art Gallery: *Industrial River Scene* by L. S. Lowry; *Notre Dame* by C. R. Nevinson.
York City, Art Gallery: *Piazza San Martino, Lucca* by Bellotto; *Sea Scape With Galliots* by Beyeren.

There are the many primitive marine paintings mentioned earlier to look out for. Also small Dutch seascapes and also English ones. One of the finest collections of marine paintings is naturally enough in the National Maritime Museum in Greenwich, London. Look especially for W. van de Velde. Turner's beautiful *Evening Star* is in the National Gallery, London, although as you may know, most of his paintings are in the Tate Gallery, London. The Tate also has paintings by Utrillo. In the National Gallery there are some of Canaletto's best paintings, also Cappelle, Goyen and Guardi.

BOOKS FOR FURTHER STUDY

In the series Studio Drawing Books, published by Studio Vista:

Buildings by Richard Downer.
Ships by John Worsley.
Painting in Towns and Cities by Hans Schwarz.

Of living painters who paint very good sea- or townscapes, the work of the following can usually be seen at the Royal Academy Summer Exhibitions:

Townscapes by Ken Howard and Carel Weight, R.A.
Seascapes by Peter Coker, A.R.A.

CHAPTER THIRTEEN

TO HELP YOUR PAINTING FURTHER

Reading through *Beginner's Guide To Painting In Oils*, it may appear that there are no rigid rules. Where possible as many alternative approaches have been suggested. Rules that work for one person do not necessarily for another. There are suggestions to start out from – when they are no longer useful to you, try something else. At first, one has to make many experiments to find out what is one's own sort of painting. Perhaps the only definite rules are: care and respect of materials, and regular work. It is much better to paint for two hours every week, rather than ten hours at a stretch when the mood takes you. Even the most professional and dedicated painters have frequently to drive themselves to start work when they are not in the mood. Once you begin the mood generates itself.

Much concerned with painting can be learned – providing one has the wish to paint. Two very great painters, Poussin and Cézanne, had very little natural facility, but by sheer force of will, became wonderful painters. Some people, do of course, have a natural facility and talent. It can be this very thing that, paradoxically, makes it so easy for them that they stop trying. Most people's difficulties are within themselves – often a fear that the painting will go wrong. This is inevitable sometimes, but others will turn out all right. At the beginning one should not be too concerned with doing a 'good' painting. One should want to paint for its own sake, as indeed, do most people who paint. Some people get unreasonably discouraged by their first efforts. There is no doubt, although it is a truism, that one does learn from one's mistakes. If one does one good painting every year, this is a satisfying proportion if one's working life is twenty-five or thirty years. This leads on to: what do we generally accept as a good painting? If one could find definitions in our common speech, they might be: vitality, oneness of concept, unity of composition and feeling. Also, something in a painting that communicates to other people. All these can be true of figurative and abstract paintings.

To come to practicalities that will help your painting further. An earlier chapter suggested carrying a sketchbook. This will train you really to use your eyes. We are taught at an early age to read, often before we are taught to observe. At first, when one draws, one is inclined to give every object one sees a name. An exercise in learning to see is, when you see an object, to draw its tone and shape!

Use photographs whenever they inspire you.

COPYING, ETC.

Perhaps some teachers would not recommend copying. You should please yourself. I find it is a marvellous way of learning. One's favourite paintings and painters are in the end one's best teachers. It is a way of trying to 'persuade' a great painting to give up its secrets as it were.

There are many ways of copying. You can do a literal copy. To do so in any gallery, you must first ask permission. Then you should get a board exactly the size of the painting, or part of the painting, you wish to copy.

You do not have to make literal copies. We are all familiar with Picasso's variations on other people's paintings. Copy by lines or tones, or by changing the colours.

Experiment at any time with new colours, providing they are permanent.

One often comes across these definitions: *amateur* and *professional*. They are usually taken to mean in the literal sense, that an amateur paints for its own sake, but a professional for a living. This generalisation is seldom accurate, though I have often found myself saying 'amateurish' when the painting looks as though the artist has cared not one bit for his equipment. This can be true of anyone.

Never be afraid of painting what you like. There is no such thing as bad subject matter, though there is such a thing as bad treatment of a subject. Every subject brings problems of painting. It is annoying, indeed, that an art critic will take a bad painting of a miner (for example) more seriously than one of flowers. It is fashionable to be scornful of the popular and the pretty. The contempt, however, always seems to come from those who do not paint.

A WORD ABOUT SCALE

This is very personal, like the way you handle your paint. It is as personal as the slope of your handwriting. Some painters by nature paint large, i.e. greater than 4 ft x 5 ft. Others paint small. There can be no rule, as the choice is often a matter of eyesight in any case. As you paint you will find your natural scale. A possible disadvantage to painting on a very large scale is the fact that such pictures may not be so readily accepted for exhibitions.

Have a timetable to work to. I find one very helpful. Every two or three months plan ahead what you mean to do and to finish in that time. Have alternatives in case something cannot be done (like planning a landscape painting and there is nothing but rain!).

Do not throw any work away for at least eighteen months. Always keep what you have done, as, however disappointing it might have seemed at the time; after a while it will look quite different. Rather than actually throw boards or canvas away if you think you do not want to re-work them, paint them over with flake white, or foundation white. This is just as good treatment for canvas too.

Another point of controversy. Always be prepared to sell your work if anyone wants it. Never give it away. Some artists may feel quite the opposite, believing it is only the decent thing to give work away to anyone who admires it. Perhaps my experiences in this direction have been unlucky, but I find that people do not appreciate paintings that are given away. It is inclined to make them think that you 'just do them' somehow.

A point mentioned in Chapter 2 about the advantage of cutting your board when you have finished a painting, to improve the composition if need be. One can do this if one is very strong minded, and does not let it become a habit. Otherwise one will get careless about composition in the first place. Or, as bad, chop one's work about so much, that nothing is left; something I was always doing when I painted on board!

Portrait commissions, or portraits of horses or pets for that matter, have a slightly different angle from a painting one sells because somebody has chosen it, already finished.

Never accept a portrait commission if the person concerned does not know your work. This is doomed to failure. However hard up you are for money, do not be tempted to take work under these conditions.

A portrait is a partnership, but with the painter as the senior partner. See that the sittings each time are not less than an hour. Overestimate the number of sittings you will need rather than otherwise. After a certain stage the sitter and his relations should have a good look at the painting. Be prepared to listen carefully to any criticisms, though the critics should formulate their criticisms into something definite, and not just vague discontent. Obviously, any one wanting drastic changes should be prepared to give you the sittings. If, after reasonable time, things are not going to work, abandon work with good grace. Settle for the cost of materials. If, however, everyone is pleased, get a good photograph taken of the painting, as this will help you obtain more work.

Animals. Successful animal painters – and this is particularly true of horse painters – see animals in a particular way. A lover of horses and somebody who really knows about them does see horses differently from other people. Horses are marvellous to draw and paint, but if one wants to please a horse lover one really has to be on their wavelength. This means seeing the horse as a painter and as a horse lover. Many people rightly love drawing the movement and rhythm of horses, but you should still practise painting every aspect. Photographs of a horse's movements arrested in motion are very useful to a painter.

At the end of this chapter is a brief glossary. However, a very useful dictionary for the artist is:

Penguin Dictionary of Art and Artists by P. and L. Murray.

A BRIEF GLOSSARY

(Mostly based on the *Oxford English Dictionary* definitions.)

AESTHETICS. Pertaining to the appreciation or criticism of the beautiful.

ALLA PRIMA. Direct painting on to the canvas or board without any thin painting first. You paint spontaneously without building up the paint gradually.

CHIAROSCURO. The balance of light and shade in a picture.

COMPOSITION. The action of putting together, or combining, the due arrangement of the parts of a picture, or other works of art.

COVERING POWER OR DENSITY. The area which a given amount of pigment will cover to give a satisfactory coating.

FORM. To give solid shape to.

GLAZE. Painting with oil colour well-thinned in oil and turpentine, or other thinner so that it is transparent. Properly a glaze should not contain white, so that it is truly transparent.

GROUND. What you put on the support, over the size. Also called priming. Can be acrylic, emulsion or oil. Usually white but can be tinted any colour.

HARMONY. Combination or adaptation of parts in related things to form a consistent and orderly whole.

HUE. Tint or quality of a particular colour.

KEEPING. In old fashioned books applied only to landscape, but applicable to any branch of painting. That the tonal values of each colour are in place to effect distance or closeness. To eliminate colours to see greater tonality, half shut your eyes when you look at anything.

LINE. A stroke or mark long in proportion to its breadth. Contour outline, or limit or boundary of an area.

MEDIUM. That which binds the powdered paint together. Or what dilutes the paint.

PRIMING. See GROUND.

SCUMBLING. The opposite of glazing. Putting opaque white-based colour over a dark ground.

SINKING. Dull patches in oil paint, caused by too absorbent ground, wrong medium, or too much dilutant. Prevention better than cure!

SIZE. A thin glue. Stops the acid in linseed oil rotting away the support. Essential on any support, unless priming is acrylic.

STIPPLE. Dabbing the brush, like a stencil. Use old or cheap brushes for this.

TRADITION. That which is handed down.

Basic vocabulary of painting equipment in other languages, in case you need them on holiday. Oil colours are named in other languages on Rowney and Winsor and Newton tubes.

ENGLISH	FRENCH	GERMAN	ITALIAN	SPANISH
Board	Panneau	Hartfaserplatte	Pannello di fibre	Tabla
Canvas	Toile imprimée	Malerleinwand	Canovaccio	Lienzo
Charcoal	Charbon de bois	Holzkohle	Carbone di legno	Carbon di lena
Colour	Couleur	Farbe	Colore	Color
Easel	Chevalet	Staffleei	Cavalletto	Caballete
Linseed Oil	Huile de Lin	Leinöl	Olio di linosa	Oleo linaza
Palette	Palette	Malerscheibe	Tavolozza	
Palette knife	Couteau	Palettemesser	Tavolozza spatola	
Paintbrush	Pinceau	Malerpinsel	Pennello	Pincel
Turpentine	Terebenthine	Terpentin	Trementima	Trementina

TAILPIECE

Finally, disagree if you wish with everything in this book, if you believe that what you are painting is right, and is what you want to do!

CHAPTER FOURTEEN

VARNISHING, FRAMING AND EXHIBITING

Varnish protects paintings. After a while all oil paintings go somewhat dull as the oil evaporates from the paint. Varnish brings out the colour again like new. No painting in a cold damp climate should be varnished until a year after completion, as, technically, the paint is not dry enough to receive it. In a hot dry climate, you can varnish paintings after six months.

To Varnish. Use a synthetic resin varnish. Both Winsor & Newton and Rowney manufacture very good synthetic clear varnish for painting. They are both quite free from the old fashioned natural resins which had a yellowish tint. The painting should be quite free of dust and dirt. The painting should be laid flat in a dust free room. The varnish should be applied in broad smooth strokes with a soft brush. An ox-hair brush does very well for this.

Some painters use retouching varnish if the paint goes dull during the process of painting. Retouching varnish has always been doubtful. Some experts believe that retouching varnish goes black in time, and I have experienced this myself. Better in the first place to use enough linseed oil with your turpentine; so that the paint does not go too dull while you are painting.

FRAMING

A frame isolates a painting from its surroundings. Even a large abstract painting should have a frame, albeit just a strip of metal. A frame makes a considerable difference to a painting, often enabling one to view it afresh. To frame paintings yourself saves a great deal of money though it must be done properly, as a bad frame is worse than useless.

The answer is to have two or three very good frames. Have them the standard sizes to which you generally work, so that the frames can be used for several pictures. A good frame can make all the difference to a painting. If it has to compete with others before a selection committee, a painting that is a borderline case stands a better chance well-framed.

CLASSES AND CLUBS

Most people want to join classes and clubs. To join a local art school or evening institute, you should write to your local education office, who will send you a list. A class or painting group is very useful if you want to work from the model. Many people find that they learn as much from the other students as from the teacher. A regular class imposes the essential discipline of regular work. Local art clubs, societies, and groups have the advantage of visiting teachers and lecturers.

PUBLICATIONS

The Artist magazine, published by The Artist Publishing Co., 33 Warwick Square, London, S.W.1 is excellent. You will find that all local art clubs advertise there. *The Artist* appears every month. Articles are on every aspect of technique and art theory. They have the added advantage of all being by practising artists. Very useful pages of advertising include artists' suppliers all over the country, art classes, and painting holidays.

Arts Review is published by Gainsborough Periodicals, Wyndham Place, London, W.1. Here you will find coverage of every exhibition in public and private galleries in the British Isles. An essential, if you want to know what is going on in the art world.

Arts Review also advertises well in advance sending-in days for national and local exhibitions. Also posts in the art world.

EXHIBITING

Start exhibiting as soon as you can. It is a very good way

of learning more about your work, seeing it together with other people's. You will see whether it really can hold its own in unfamiliar surroundings. Also, of course, if you are thinking of making a name for yourself in the art world, this is the way it is done. Do not lose heart if you are rejected quite a bit at first. It is exceedingly unlikely that your work will be thrown out for being no good at all. The most likely reason is that it is a borderline case and has to compete with many on about the same level. Of course, it may be very good and the selection committee may have made an error of judgement. But if you are rejected from an exhibition, go along and see what the sort of standard is. You will learn something by so doing. On no account give up. Try next time and try others. It is an idea to start showing in local shows, working up to national shows. Very local shows will be advertised in your local paper or public library.

For a small fee, the Art Exhibition Bureau at 6 Suffolk Street, Pall Mall, London, S.W.1 will keep you posted about exhibitions. You then fill in a postcard of the ones for which you want the sending-in forms, and they will send them. A very useful service.

Here is a list of national and local exhibitions. *Arts Review* also advertises national and local competitions.

This list does not include the water colour exhibitions, or anything other than oil paint.

You can live anywhere if you want to send in to the following:

National Society
Paris Salon (you can send in through agents)
Royal Society of Portrait Painters
Flower Painters
Royal Society of Marine Artists
Industrial Painters
Royal Institute of Oil Painters
Royal Scottish Academy
Royal Society of British Artists
Pictures for Schools

New English Art Club
Society of Wild Life Artists
International Amateur Art
Royal West of England Academy

You have to live in the area to send in to the following:

Aberdeen Artists' Society
Manchester Academy
Royal Glasgow Institute
Society of Scottish Artists
Yorkshire Artists
Royal Birmingham Society of Artists

You can see that apart from even more localised shows, there is quite a selection, and it will be only a question of trying hard enough, and you are bound to start showing soon. Quite the most popular exhibition of all for every artist is the Royal Academy, London. In the last three years or so, it represented some of the best in British painting, work that can hold its own with the best galleries in Europe and America. Work submitted to the Royal Academy must be well framed.

Private Galleries: Apart from the Royal Academy, artists' reputations can be made in private galleries. If you want to try your work in them, you have to take paintings to see the owner of any gallery that looks as though it might show the kind of work you do.

This is a bit alarming at first, but if you get a dealer interested, he will then probably come to see you. If a dealer tells you he is booked up for two years ahead, so much the better; any reputable gallery should normally be. At first, a dealer may take one or two paintings for a mixed show. A dealer will take 33⅓ per cent of sale price as a rule.

Other possibilities of showing your work: Public libraries, local craft shops, even hotels. Open air shows.

Prints: Publishers of prints advertise for paintings. It is a good idea to try sending colour slides of your paintings. You never know, yours may be chosen.

Some other suggestions: Keep a note book of the following:

favourite mixtures for colours you have discovered (Sickert kept elaborate notes of this kind); quotations from artists' letters and sayings that appeal to you; poems or anything else that inspires your work.

If you work from photographs: Keep folders under subject matter, e.g. sport, animals, racing cars etc. Always add to them. In the newspapers, one regularly sees the most fascinating photographs of sport or racing etc., forming very good compositions for paintings. Be sure to cut them out regularly. Keep careful account of work that you sell and be sure that you keep track of where it has gone. In case you do get involved with problems of taxation, you should be sure also to keep all material and framing bills. In any case, it is a good habit.

The following suggestion might be classed as a thoroughly bad habit but . . ! Start collecting oddments for still lifes. Pots and containers that take your fancy. Pieces of cloth as backgrounds for any painting are worth having a collection to choose from.

Some artists find all kinds of odd objects inspiring, whether they intend to paint them or not. The prime example of course is Rembrandt, whose ever-searching intelligence inquired into everything from tropical shells to classical antiquity. On the subject of finding things like jugs and crocks in junk shops, keep an eye open for the following equipment that is now no longer manufactured:

Studio easels; a dark mirror (called a Claude Lorraine Glass, though it is not known whether he used one) that eliminates colour and only reflects back tone; the fine old boxes made for keeping equipment; wooden frames, not as cheap as they were but well worth getting; old stretchers from canvases that have had to be re-stretched.

CHAPTER FIFTEEN

PAINTING AND RELATED STUDIES

If one paints, it will lead one to question and speculate about the external world and one's own inner world. Leonardo da Vinci believed that a painting should be a cosmology of knowledge. Maybe it was because he was first a painter, trained to use his eyes, that led to his amazing researches into the natural world. From Leonardo's day until Cézanne, painting in Western Europe was considered a science. Two great aspects of scientific knowledge developed through painting. They are anatomy and perspective. Till very recently they were compulsory studies in art school. They are still worth study. Anatomy is not only about man, it applies of course to all living things. From a practical point of view, anatomy is valuable in painting animals. So many animals are painted as kinds of pets with human attributes. Animal anatomy helps us really look at them. Fig. 97 shows the horse and man skeleton from the Natural History Museum.

Anatomy is directly related to function.

As in birds and fishes (Fig. 98).

The movement of muscles has often fascinated artists. A knowledge of muscles makes us see the subtlest change and nuance of movement (Fig. 99).

Anatomy is also about living things and growth. Plants reflect the basic patterns in the universe (Fig. 100).

PERSPECTIVE

We take perspective so much for granted in Western Europe, that it is difficult for us to see now how intensely exciting it must have been when it was discovered. It is a kind of mathematics. When perspective was formulated, mathematical knowledge was not nearly so advanced as it is

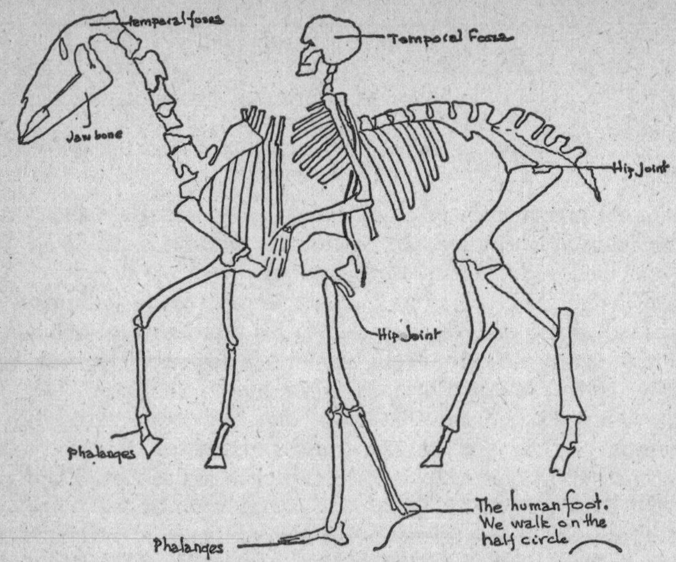

Fig. 97 Man and horse. Man, the only upright-standing animal.

today, so, when a painter used perspective it indeed appeared that art and science were one. Perspective was a means, too, of ordering our perception of the phenomena of nature. One could create a microcosm of the universe. Leonardo discovered and gave name to aerial perspective. This in effect is the appearance of things in distance and air. The fact that distances look blue, and objects in the distance lose their sharpness. Aerial perspective and its development are possible because of the nature of oil paint. Distances, of course, are not blue in fact. They appear blue because we see them that way. The way we see and the way our eyes work has become of increasing interest to painters during the last hundred or more years. Many art schools now teach psychological and physiological aspects of vision, rather than anatomy or perspective. So here is a few words about these factors:

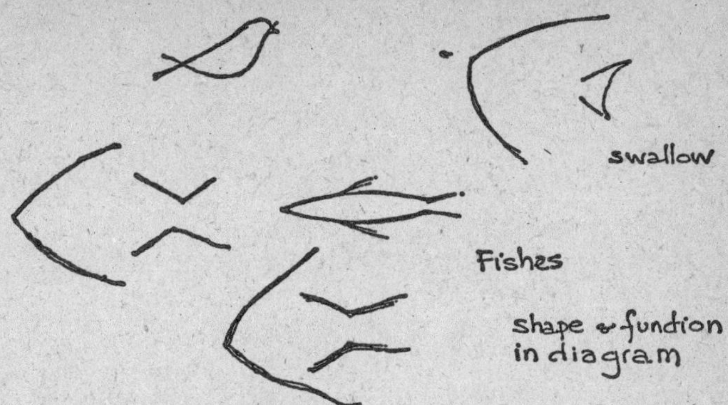

Fig. 98 Birds and fishes.

Psychology of Vision. Seeing and knowing. Psychology of vision asks and attempts to answer many questions. How do we see? What conditions our vision? Do we now see differently from people in the past? It is certain that we do. We may look at a Byzantine fresco figure and admire it as a humorous picture. When it was painted, however, it was certainly 'read' quite differently. This involves what we expect from a painting or an artist in the first place. It is certain, too, that we pick up unconscious attitudes, like our interpretation of light and shadow into solid form. Paintings open our eyes and condition our vision. Many of us 'see' colour in shadows after studying Impressionist paintings. Most people looked at sunflowers for the first time after seeing a Van Gogh painting of them. What can be in literal fact a scumble of flake white on a canvas, we see as cloud or piece of fabric. Is there some deep-down cause that makes us see 'eyes' in wood-grain, or 'faces' in frost patterns on the window? Can we unlearn knowledge? Like seeing a bundle of blankets that we take to be a sleeping person; on learning that it is only blankets, you can never recapture your first impression of the object. Do we paint within a tradition that conditions our seeing? Is our experimental art in terms of tradition? Does conscious rejection of tradition

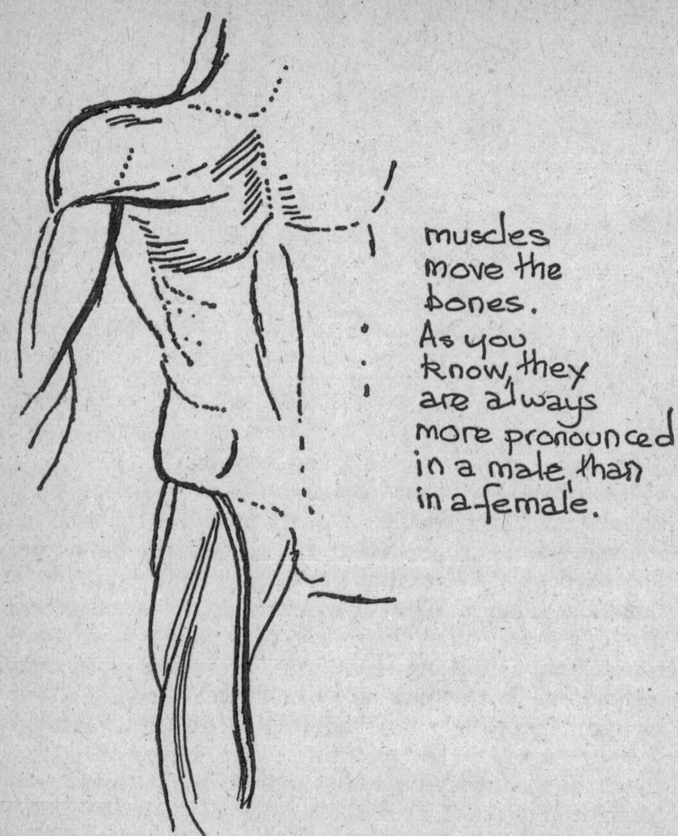

Fig. 99 Muscles.

imply knowledge of that tradition? Could we see a down-trodden, bloated deaf old man as an infinitely noble creature, had it not been for Rembrandt's self portraits? These are only a few of the questions that the psychology of vision asks, and in, many cases explains. Psychology of vision is almost inseparable from:

Physiology of Vision. This is more concerned with the

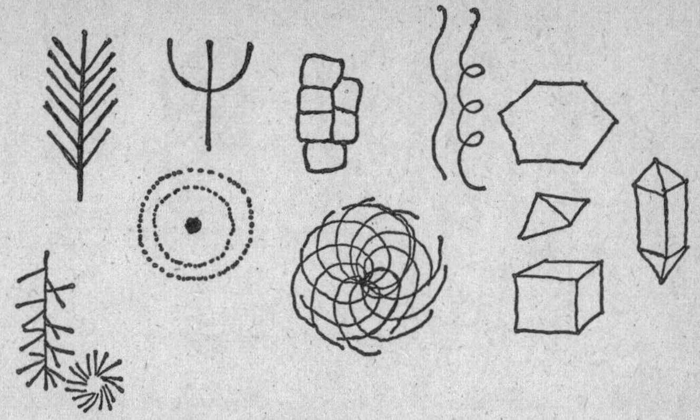

Fig. 100 Basic universal patterns from plants, crystals and molecular structures.

mechanics of the eye. Obvious examples are optical illusions. It is certain that our eyes are agitated by these images in a way that our brain registered effects that are not there. This has been explored in the paintings of Vasarely and Bridget Riley. This is a curious instance of where it is difficult for our mind to control our eyes. We know that optical illusions are in front of us but we still see them, even if we try not to. This book has mentioned many times the effects of complementary colours. Take a red patch on a grey ground – the grey will appear greenish without the green being there in fact. Then there is the phenomenon of after-images. What you see after looking at something and then shutting your eyes? Depending on how vividly you see after-images, you can make all kinds of experiments with them. Just by looking at anything, and shutting your eyes, you can see light images, negative, and positive, that your conscious mind has played no part in selecting. There are many excellent textbooks on the subject that can explain why the retina behaves in certain ways, and a selection will be listed at the end of the chapter. Light, of course, affects the brain, and our actions. It may be, then, that the external world, which we see in

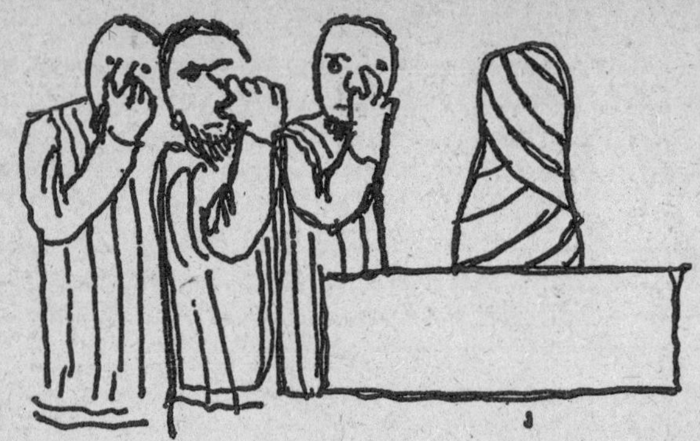

Fig. 101 From the 'Raising of Lazarus' in a Byzantine fresco, Moraĉka, Montenegro.

terms of light, can so affect our brain that it acts upon us to paint.

AESTHETICS

One of the finest and noblest characteristics of the European tradition is that an artist is more than a skilled craftsman. He is creating works that stand with the highest achievements of literature and philosophy. The branch of philosophy that asks the question and speculates on things that concern the artist is aesthetics. But here we run into a difficulty. Aesthetics assumes that one is interested in beauty in the first place. The great classic painters, like Raphael, Titian, Poussin, etc., never questioned this. The painter was expected to create ideal beauty. Most major painting of the twentieth century has ignored this; many painters believe that ideas of the beautiful are merely irrelevant. Perhaps in the last century beauty had been so debased into nauseating sentimentality, that we are most likely still suffering from reaction, to the extent that ugliness is said to be more 'real' and more truthful than beauty. It is certainly easier from a practical point of view to paint the ugly. One can have the justification that it is more 'real'. Realism in art sometimes has a social bias, taking the attitude that this is what life is about. In fact it is scarcely true, except in a few cases. Most people are in some way or another concerned with beauty. This can take many aspects. One of the most obvious is gardening. Another is dressing children in cheerful colours. Many philosophers and painters in the past have discussed beauty. They question whether it has unchanging content, and whether the nature of beauty can be defined. Here are some quotations on beauty you may find inspiring. They may also start you off into reading further.

The method and nature of the aesthetics as we understand it in Europe, was adopted to a very large extent from the Greeks. To quote from Plato:

'The principle of goodness has reduced itself to the law of beauty. For measure and proportion always pass into beauty and excellence.'

St. Thomas Aquinas wrote in his vast *Summa*: 'Beauty includes three conditions; integrity or perfection, since things that are imperfect are by that very fact ugly; due proportion or harmony; and lastly brightness and clarity.'

To generalise to the point of rashness, the Italian painters of the sixteenth and seventeenth centuries, believed in an ultimate ideal beauty. This may not come into our scheme of things today, but it helps us understand the art of that time. Aesthetics to some philosophers are questions of taste, a property of the mind, as separate from the body. To others, aesthetics involves taste. The very word taste admitting to a quality of the senses. Perhaps our response to beauty is in what we want to touch, feel, and eat.

Collect your own quotations on the beautiful, if you find it helps you paint. Unless of course, you feel, like Camille Pissarro (called by Cézanne, 'the humble and colossal'), who wrote to his son in terms suggesting that aesthetics were romantic trickery. I cannot agree with this assessment, but this book is about YOUR painting!

One cannot pretend that beauty is the only content of art or life, but aesthetics often questions the moral content of beauty: whether beauty relates to what is good. It is finally moral force that raises great works of art above the others and ensures their survival. It is this moral force that gives those parts of experience, like suffering and death, the quality that prevents them from ugliness and cruelty in art.

ART HISTORY

After looking at paintings, one will probably want to know a bit more about them. This is where art history enlarges one's knowledge of painting. Painting, of course, is only a part of the whole process of man's works, which include architecture, design and sculpture. In studying art history one finds one is discovering about all other aspects of history, and how world events affect the process of art. A very good beginning to art history, is to ask; What was this painting for? A Flemish altar piece was painted for a quite different reason from, for example, a Boucher nude. History of art has many faces. To some art historians, it has been the social necessity of art. To others the economics of art, or to put it crudely: who paid for it. Perhaps you have your own interpretation. You can look for fashions in clothes or beauty. Or a history of methods and techniques. Our concept of history are other aspects of the European tradition. We can ask if what we paint now will affect the future, or is it dependent on the past. Perhaps art history could even be about the ways people saw the external world in past ages, or indeed, like science, the history of the way man interprets nature. Art history teaches tolerance. A knowledge of history is the preservation of freedom. The first act of tyranny is the abolition of history.

SOME PRACTICAL APPROACHES TO LEARNING ART HISTORY:

By themes. Follow up through the ages the way artists approach their subject matter, i.e. portraits, landscape etc. A very good subject is something like the condition of man. You could start with Breughel's peasants, Rembrandt's characters, Goya's appalling paintings of war, and so on.

This of course will lead you to background reading, which is just as it should be.

By the characters of countries. England or France or what you will.

Famous people and their times.

Methods and Techniques. A practical approach, whereby you will learn a lot about painting.

Or some method your own, that I have not thought of. For all this, however, there are some very good painters to whom the process of art history is irrelevant. They have favourite paintings or painters, and this is about as far as it goes. As long as paintings give you pleasure and enlarge your vision of things, that is really all that matters.

Even if the complexities of art history are not within your scheme of things, and your vision is of favourite paintings just as they are; the lives of artists may be inspiring. To many, this is the best part of art history, the actual lives of the artists. Everyone is surely familiar with the life of Vincent Van Gogh, from general knowledge as much as any other source. His whole inner and outward life is revealed in his letters to his brother Theo. They are continually inspiring reading. Van Gogh appeared desperately to want to lead a normal life, like other people. Maybe his recognition of the normal is why his paintings have come into the common experience of all of us. We all know his little boats, potato eaters, boots, blossom trees, etc. Another artist we know about from legend is Gauguin. Perhaps some of us have a secret longing to up and away to paint in the south seas. Remember, though, that legends and popularisations of artists' lives are rather inclined to understate one vital thing: the relentless hard work of these artists.

As always, I end this chapter with a book list. Obviously, any comprehensive one would end by being a bibliography in many volumes. The books recommended here are to start you finding books for yourselves.

ANATOMY, ETC.

Anatomy For Artists by E. Wolff. Lewis Medical Publishers.

Knowing and Drawing Trees by Adrian Hill. Blandford Press.

Artistic Anatomy of Trees by R. Vicat Cole. Dover Books (New York but obtainable in Britain).

On Growth and Form by D'Arcy Thomson. Cambridge Paper Back.

MORE ABOUT PERSPECTIVE

The Birth and Rebirth of Pictorial Space by John White. Faber and Faber.

THE PSYCHOLOGY OF VISION AND THE PHYSIOLOGY OF VISION

Art and Visual Perception by Rudolph Arnheim. Faber and Faber.

The Psychology of Perception by M. D. Vernon. Penguin Books.

Art and Illusion by E. H. Gombrich. Phaidon Press.

AESTHETICS

The Theory of Beauty by E. F. Carritt. Metheun.

ART HISTORY

There are a vast number of books under this heading but two indispensable to start with are:

The Story of Art by E. H. Gombrich. Phaidon Press.

Civilisation by Kenneth Clark. John Murray.

A student once complained that the two above named works were simple. The answer to this is, so is the slow movement of Beethoven's *Quartet in A Minor*, opus 132. If you have already read these books, read them again!

CHAPTER SIXTEEN

SUMMING UP

If the thought of more philosophy and contemplation is too much, by all means ignore this chapter and start painting.

Many people are diffident about painting for the same reason. A lot of people have a feeling that painting may not be 'useful,' either to do full or part time. How many artists once suffered disapproving family, or well meaning head teachers' attempts to divert their talents in other directions. In the way of being primarily useful or productive, painting is not like farming or nursing. Most of us have seen or read George Orwell's *1984*. As a protest against cruelty, lies, and the all-powerful state, the hero, Winston Smith, starts to write a journal. We know, from the start, that Smith is doomed to be found out by the State, then tortured and killed. Yet how much, as we read *1984* do we long for Smith to write his journal. For the very reason that it is his, and it is a private and personal expression of something almost indefinable. Perhaps painting has a value for these reasons. Winston Smith felt perhaps that by his small and wretched effort he might communicate to others, and to some future time. We feel when reading this, that something creative is of intense importance.

Apart from this, one paints as much as any other reason because one's talents lie in this direction. I have heard a number of times statements saying that a craft is more 'honest' than painting and that graphics are more practical. Of course this is rubbish. A typographic designer responds to printing, and a potter to clay, because of something within them, not to exclude anything else.

TO TAKE YOU FURTHER

The last few years have seen the growth of pop music.

Here, groups and individuals get together, and, sometimes even spontaneously, create marvellous and inventive tunes that reach thousands of people. Other people open shops of their own to make original and beautiful clothes. By this same right, anyone who wants to paint should do so. We often see quite good paintings that we feel we could equal, so why not try? Remember, most difficulties are within, and every difficulty can be surmounted somehow. At no time in history has established art been more out of touch with ordinary folk. Much of gallery art is downright unpleasant, much else seems to take the modern art joke to the point of no return. Most, at any rate, has no moral direction, and has completely abandoned any standards of good or bad. This is where, now more than ever, you, me or anyone should paint things that are expressing something that is our own; and something that is for our family and friends.

Now let us finish with a few more quotations from the artists of the past.

Inevitably the quotations are taken out of context. This, and a personal choice, rather prejudices the meaning, but reading them here may inspire you to read the originals for yourself in full. Or indeed inspire you to look around at new things, books, poetry, music, and people. The value of any work of art, great or small, is that it increases our awareness and experience. It can be a Raphael *Madonna*, that is a miracle of purely formal values, yet is in our basic life, the mother and child. Our mind can be enriched by a small anonymous still life. Many people complain of the uniformity of contemporary life. This is when we should start painting.

The universe you are creating within the four edges of the board is very valuable. When we hear a beautiful song by an anonymous or forgotten composer, we feel that it was worth his whole life's work for that one song. Never be put off. One gets depressed – one paints. Maybe this is the opposite part of creating. Perhaps it is somebody painting away who must fill a canvas who may bring back a visual art that it is at all levels of experience. Like Raphael's *Madonna*, and

Constable's *Hay Wain*. Some people find these paintings obvious, but the borderline between the true and the commonplace is very narrow. The subtlety of the obvious is understood in science; it can also be understood in painting. The simplest peasant will have an object of beauty for its own sake. So do most people. A need for beauty is a first need. We must paint to communicate with others. This will keep your humour. Remember to keep your favourite paintings and visual images always around you. Look around at your fellow men, and try to see what is eternal in people at all times. In life as in works of literature.

Much of what I have written has been taken consciously or unconsciously from what I have been taught. One learns consciously and unconsciously. When one teaches, one hands down what one has learned. Teaching is part of tradition. It has an ancestry and continuance. What we do now is of the past and becomes the future. This is how the tradition of Europe will go on in painting. Not in established galleries, but, through unknown persons painting.

If you paint, you may feel that what you have in mind to paint has been done many times before. This is every reason to paint them. Perhaps there are eternal forms that each generation has to interpret afresh. These eternal forms may be the cylinder, the sphere and the cone that Cézanne wrote about. Or some aspect of the human figure. Can we find basic forms that are true in art at all times? We can try to find them. It is this search that makes us paint. Painting can be learned, providing you want to paint. In the end you will do good paintings. The unfortunate painters who fail are generally those who may have visions of themselves as geniuses. Not as painters, painting for its own sake.

Blake wrote: 'What has art to do with reason?'

Bonnard wrote: 'Colour has logic its own, no less strict than that of forms,' and again, 'When I am painting I try to keep a firm grip on the original idea, but if I'm weak and let go, I lose touch with the first visual experience.'

C. Pissarro wrote: 'The more toilsome the work, the stronger you will emerge from it.'

Kandinsky wrote: 'The artist is not only justified in using, but is under a moral obligation to use, only those forms which fulfil his own need.'

Matisse wrote: 'I cannot copy nature in a servile way. I must interpret nature, and submit it to the spirit of the picture,' and again, 'the chief aim of colour should be to serve expression as well as possible.'

From Palma Giovanni's description of Titian's method of working: 'But the climax of his retouching he effected by blurring the outlines of the highlights with the tips of his fingers, to bring them to half tints, and melting one colour into another.'

Constable: 'When I sit down to make a sketch from nature, the first thing I try to do is to forget I have ever seen a picture,' also 'Willows, old rotten planks, slimy posts, I love such things. Those things make me a painter and I am glad . . .' 'I never saw an ugly thing in my life.'

Poussin: 'Coarse or vile subjects are the refuge of those who, by reason of the weakness of their talent cannot choose anything else.'

Leonardo da Vinci: 'The divinity inherent in the science of painting raises the painter's spirit to her own level,' and 'Nature is full of infinite causes that were never set forth in experience.'

Paul Klee: 'Art does not reproduce the visible, rather, it makes visible,' and 'Pictures look at us.'

Grandma Moses, the American primitive painter: 'My father would get me and my brother white paper by the sheet. He liked seeing us do pictures; it was a penny a sheet, and it lasted longer than candy.'

Van Gogh: 'In future I am going to use black and white boldly in my palette, just as they are . . . they are colours, their simultaneous contrast is as striking as that of red and green.' Also, 'I enjoyed doing this Seurat-like interior. With flat tints brushed on roughly, with thick impasto, walls pale lilac, ground faded broken red, washbasin blue. By means of all these very diverse tones I have wanted to express absolute restfulness.'

FINAL TAILPIECE

You may have got so far. Where to go next? Only go on. One hears the commonplace that artists crave recognition. Some do. But most painters only want to go on with their painting. It is a misrepresentation to think that some very great artists were quite unrecognised in their lifetime, only to receive acclaim after their death. This is not quite the way it is. Most painters who time has shown to be great, were recognised in their lifetime. This, was, however, by people who had discrimination, cared for paintings, but, like the rest of us, did not very often, if ever, have the few spare guineas to buy all the paintings they liked. As well as paint, we might even recognise a great painting. Where though, you will still be asking, do I go next? Rembrandt was continually asked that by his pupil Hoogstraten. Rembrandt's answer, in a sentence, will tell you how to go on: 'Paint what you know, then you will come to learn soon enough those hidden things about which you ask.'

INDEX

Also by Barbara Dorf in Sphere Books

A GUIDE TO WATER COLOUR PAINTING

The fact that water colours are simple to use, quick-drying and comparatively cheap gives them a great advantage, and, for the novice and expert alike, the author describes in detail how the techniques for many styles of water colour painting, from landscape and still life to portrait and abstract, can be developed. Extensive information is given on the materials used – the many types of brushes and paper – and for more adventurous work the use of inks and wax crayons is also covered.

This book is a guide in the truest sense, as it lays down no rigid rules, but instead offers practical advice that leaves readers free to experiment and express themselves with water colours in their own way.

0 7221 3027 9 75p

More Practical Handbooks in Sphere

THE GUIDE TO PRACTICAL PHOTOGRAPHY

JOHN WASLEY

The Guide to Practical Photography is an excellent handbook for every amateur striving to be that much more of a professional.

With John Wasley's expert help you can discover which type of camera to buy for your particular kind of photography, what the various lenses and meters do and how to use them, and how to match the right film to the subject for optimum results. Processing and dark room techniques are simplified and explained to enable you to get first-class results. How to find the best developer to use for any given film, how to expose in an enlarger, selecting the best enlarging paper and a host of other important topics are just some of the essential questions answered.

Whatever kind of camera you own – a simple cartridge-load or the latest gleaming creation from Japan – this is the book for you.

Fully illustrated

0 7221 8920 6 75p

BEGINNERS GUIDE TO DO-IT-YOURSELF

TONY WILKINS and RON GRACE

Have you ever wanted to tile a bathroom, divide a room into two or build a wardrobe? Suffered with damp or draughts or needed to paint the outside of a house? Advice on these and many more is in this extremely practical book. Covering all aspects of home maintenance from hiring the tools for the job to wiring a plug, it will help keep your home safe and comfortable. Both the absolute beginner and the more proficient man or woman about the house will find this book an invaluable addition to their shelves – when they've built them!

0 7221 9142 1 50p

BEGINNERS GUIDE TO HOUSE PLANTS

VIOLET STEVENSON

The new and easily understandable approach to the subject of house plants made in this book follows a logical progression, for the beginner is introduced to the plants in related groups, beginning with those that are easiest to cultivate in the average home. As each group is discussed in detail the logic of the treatment required to keep them in good health becomes apparent and the reader achieves a new understanding of plants which greatly simplifies their care. It also enables the widest range of plants to be introduced into the house successfully.

The beginner with house plants can tend her charges with confidence and assurance with this book beside her, and the more experienced enthusiast will gain new interest from the obvious knowledge and love of plants shown by the author.

0 7221 8156 6 45p

A Guide to Survival Today

ON NEXT TO NOTHING

Self-sufficiency on a low budget

THOMAS and SUSAN HINDE

With natural resources dwindling rapidly throughout the world, supplies of many everyday items – from glass jars to razor blades to sugar – cannot last for ever. Prompted by current inflation and gloomy forecasts for the future, more and more people are looking for ways to maintain a comfortable living standard while spending less of their hard-earned money.

On Next to Nothing is an invaluable guide to just how that can be achieved. It's not written for the fortunate few with enough land to cut themselves off from society and become completely self-sufficient. Instead, it's a book that shows how anyone, whether city- or country-dweller, can use their own skills to cut the cost of living and ensure a better future.

0 7221 4558 6 £1.25